THE EMPIRES OF IMAGE

REVEALED

T.M. KYMALAINEN

© Copyright 2011 – T. M. KYMALAINEN

Published by:

Time to Return Ministries LLC

Willow Spring, North Carolina

E-mail: timetoreturn@gmail.com

www.timetoreturnministries.com

Cover design by TTR, Publishing division; E-mail: ttrinfo@gmail.com

ISBN: 978-0-9819871-1-8

All rights reserved. This book is protected under the copyright laws. This book may not be copied or reprinted for commercial gain or profit. The use of short quotations or occasional page copying for personal or group study is permitted and encouraged. Permission will be granted upon request.

Unless otherwise indicated, all Scripture quotations are from the King James Version (KJV) of the Bible, Public domain, no permission necessary for use of Scripture.

The following translations are also occasionally cited:

Scripture quotations marked "NKJV™" are taken from the New King James Version®. Copyright © 1982 by Thomas Nelson, Inc. Used by permission. All rights reserved.

Scripture quotations marked (ESV) are from The Holy Bible, English Standard Version® (ESV®), copyright © 2001 by Crossway, a publishing ministry of Good News Publishers. Used by permission. All rights reserved.

Contrary to the common practice of English grammar, the word "satan" shall not be capitalized in this book, other than when using it in direct quotations of scripture.

ACKNOWLEDGEMENTS

My acknowledgements are quite simple, and through their simplicity I hope to pay tribute to the most amazing and wonderful One of all.

Thank you HaShem, for everything!

HaShem is a Jewish/Hebrew name for God; it means "The Name".

Speaking of names and Hebrew identities, the anglicized name of "Jesus" is used interchangeably in this book alongside the original Hebrew name for the Messiah, "Yeshua"; the Salvation of God.

TK
In the weeks before Purim, 5771

CONTENTS

One	The Nation Vs. the Empire	1
Two	Starting Off	19
Three	Behold, The Dreamer!	35
Four	Another Look	49
Five	What Can a statue Do?	57
Six	Babylon, Always With the Babble	61
Seven	Persia, More than Just Great Carpets	77
Eight	Greece, It's Certainly Not a Health Food	89
Nine	The Roaming Roman	101
Ten	"A Couple of Real Heels?"	107
Eleven	The Summer is Nigh	113
Twelve	But Wait, There's More!	121
Thirteen	Heads Up!	125

FROM THE PROVERBS OF

KING SOLOMON:

"It is the glory of God to conceal things, but the glory of kings is to search things out." (Proverbs 25:2)

PREFACE

Wars, deceitfulness, wickedness, and corruptions of all manner are rampant upon the earth in this day, and not surprisingly, they long have been. In fact, evil has been present in human life nearly as long as mankind has walked upon the earth.

In the coming pages we will attempt to sort out why such depravity is, and has been, so overwhelmingly evident among the children of Adam even though man was created in the image of the Holy God, and despite the fact that the righteous King Messiah has been given all power over all things in heaven and in the earth.

As the following two verses indicate, man was, indeed, made in the image of God; and Jesus, the last Adam, was given all power in heaven and in earth.

> *"And God said, Let us make man in our image, after our likeness: and let them have dominion over the fish of the sea, and over the fowl of the air, and over the cattle, and over all the earth, and over every creeping thing that creepeth upon the earth. (Genesis 1:26-27)*

> *"And Jesus came and spake unto them, saying, All power is given unto me in heaven and in earth." (Matthew 28:18)*

Simply put, the two questions that really need answering are: "What has happened to bespoil mankind?" and, "Why has it happened?"

The obvious answer to both of these questions is that sin came into the existence of mankind. The clear solution to this problem is redemption, which is the liberation and return of the captive from an unwanted situation. We are much too familiar with the, sadly, all too obvious problem, and given the dire and most evident consequences which the problem produces we certainly need to better familiarize ourselves with the solution.

There are many biblically accurate and fascinating ways to look at the subject of redemption; it is a key biblical issue after all, and one which is presented throughout the pages of scripture in a variety of richly illustrated ways.

However, if we are to receive a deeper understanding of the solution called redemption we must first come to realize who and what we are redeemed from. With that said, we will attempt to focus in on the redemption of man by delving into the causes and instigators of the fall of man, and specifically, on the reasons for the constant presence of everyday sin and the resulting separation from God found so commonly throughout the ranks of all mankind.

It was sin which first allowed satan's cabal access into mankind's communal existence. And, those same satanic conspirators: the principalities, and powers, and the rulers of the darkness of this world *(Ephesians 6:12)* use man's sin, and its continuing painful effects, to ensure that mankind remains separated from the Holy God as they exercise their unrelenting influence and power over Adam's children to enable spiritual wickedness to remain in its place of governance over mankind.

The biblically infamous king of Babylon, Nebuchadnezzar, was given great insight (much of it firsthand knowledge) into the workings of sin and spiritual wickedness. His dreams, specifically, have taught us much about the subjects in question; and with the help of the Lord, and the prophet Daniel, one of Nebuchadnezzar's dreams in particular will teach us yet more. They will greatly expose the lies of the adversary which pervade the earth through the attempts of the wicked to defile the everyday world around us.

Let's find out what's going on...

CHAPTER ONE

THE NATION VS THE EMPIRE

There has been a conflict raging in the realm of mankind; one of absolutely astounding proportions. This conflict is in the area of human government and focuses on how, if at all, people should be overseen within their lives and societies. It has, as all proper conflicts inevitably do, two starkly opposing ideals facing off against each other and they both have markedly different modes of conduct...

One design of governance is established by God, and it seeks to keep the continuity of truth in man's life as it carries on the manner of rule first established by the Almighty within his own heavens. This original path of life can be called the "family".

The family is a way of life built upon love, familial ties, and mutually beneficial relationships. This structure of governance is designed in holiness to build, protect, and strengthen the children of Adam through natural bonds of kinship as they sojourn upon the earth.

In this format the individual is able grow and develop; to learn, work, and give of his or her own self voluntarily. In so doing, the voluntary actions of individuals inevitably come to benefit society as a whole. This is the Godly design for order and it leads to a constructive and harmonious way of life.

The other path of governance is evil in origin, and it seeks to enforce the rule of the seemingly more powerful over all others. This design of government is one both epitomized and championed by satan. He is a twisted being who has long fancied himself to be the, *"strong man" (Mark 3:27)*, one able to enforce his will upon all others, feigning contempt of any force or law. His is a format which states: "Might makes right."

This way of rule is to be called "empire". The "empire" is built upon deceit, lust, and control. It is designed to both enchant and enslave all those who fall prey to its demonic deceptions.

The empire gives an individual two choices: one, join me and become one who serves evil and lives for self interest, or two, become my victim as I rapaciously pillage the lives of those in my path.

In this form of government the individual learns to "take" in order to succeed and the enforced servitude of others is seen as bringing about a (fleeting) form of success. This is the satanic design for human government and it leads to a destructive way of life for all involved with it.

The fall of Adam pits these two very different forms of life government into a constant striving for dominance in the world of the fallen man, with each form tenaciously gripping to the shattered remnants of mankind's now broken heart. Empire, though, claims a distinct superficial advantage.

Let's see if we can learn a bit more about each design of life:

THE FAMILY
(NATION)

On the one hand there is the "nation". The nation is a construct of Godly design and is the fourth and final level of the familial construct. It is both offshoot and part of the family unit.

All of the Godly forms of life government mentioned in scripture are simply various degrees of blood ties, of kinship; and the nation is no exception. This design of life which God had bestowed unto mankind basically sees, and keeps, the peoples of the earth ordered into a number of very large and uniquely gifted families called "nations".

How many of these large families are there?

Biblically speaking, there is a set total of seventy of these national family groups created by God to inhabit the earth. These are scripturally known as the "seventy nations" of the earth. The first time the progenitors of these nations are all mentioned together in a single chapter of the Bible is in the tenth chapter of Genesis which speaks of the sons of Noah saying, *"...and unto them were sons born after the flood"*.

These, *"sons", that* were later named in this tenth chapter were the fathers of the seventy nations which, biblically, still bear their names. Each forefather had a nation arise from his children; those unique nations would eventually come to fill the earth with the seed of Adam. In so doing, they would fulfill God's command to Adam which said: *"Be fruitful and multiply; fill the earth and subdue it" (Genesis 1:28)* NKJV™.

This tenth chapter of Genesis ends with the thirty-second verse stating:

> *"These [are] the families of the sons of Noah, after their generations, in their nations: and by these were the nations divided in the earth after the flood."*

In Numbers 29:12-34, we can get another, albeit slightly clandestine, glimpse of the seventy nations spoken of together in one chapter. In the biblically instituted Feast of the LORD known as Sukkot (or Tabernacles) God commands his nation of priests, Israel, to do an interesting thing: He commands Israel to enter into its priestly function and offer up seventy bullocks as a sacrifice unto Him.

The people of Israel have long realized that these particular offerings were on behalf of the seventy nations of the earth. One bullock was offered per nation per year. This offering was to cover the sins of the nations and afford them the ability to yet live upon the earth despite their shortcomings and sin.

For the curious, this long held Jewish understanding can be found mentioned in Midrash Rabbah, Numbers Rabbah 21:24, among other places. God in His perfection and thoroughness had Israel sacrifice just the correct and corresponding number of bullocks: seventy; one for each of the seventy nations of the earth.

In rabbinic Jewish traditions of biblical scholarship these seventy nations can be seen as the full image of the "body of Adam". Each nation represents a certain particular trait or characteristic of our father Adam, and when all nations are viewed as a whole the full likeness of Adam, the original man, can be seen.

In this biblical concept, each nation carries its own uniquely given "Adamic" anointing with it and is charged with bringing it forth into the earth. This national anointing is an attribute of blessing which is meant to benefit not only that particular national family, but to also come to the benefit of the entire "Adamic family" as a whole.

This biblically revealed train of thought, which teaches us the distinctiveness of each nation, is meant to bring about an appreciation for the uniqueness inherent to each national/family group, and to cause a thankfulness to arise within creation for the existence of the rich plurality of life found in the Godly design.

Indeed, everything created by God has this plurality of life inherently built into it which is designed to increase the quality and richness of the overall creation.

For example: there are men and there are women, there are old and there are young, there are fast decision makers and there are slow ones. And, there are the seventy nations which were given unto us to enrich our lives, our cultures, our thoughts, our economies, and our worship.

The Godly concept of "one body, but many parts" is thus seen in operation from the earliest days of human life. *(Romans 12:4; 1 Corinthians 12:12)*

In fact, to find an example which further ties the concept of "one body, but many parts" into our look at the nations representing the full body of Adam we need search no further than the Hebrew language and its word for nation, which is "goy".

"Goy" does mean nation, but it also carries with it another underlying meaning, that of "body". In this line of simile the nation is a body of people who are seen as one unit, as one corporate entity. However, we can also see the word "goy" showing us that the nations, the "goy" in entirety, are one corporate body, that of Adam's, the original man.

This dual meaning harkens back to God's original design of unity for His children. All people, as individually gifted as they may be, are still together in this existence as the body of Adam upon the earth.

All people are together as the "body of Adam"; all, that is, but one. The one people group not included with the seventy natural nations is Israel. In fact, so significant and unusual is Israel and its inception, existence, and future that its supernatural establishment through Abraham caused it to have a unique position in the earth.

Israel is the one and only true nation that is not scripturally numbered among the other seventy natural nations. It is, in fact, a nation which dwells alone; and it is not counted among the nations. *(Numbers 23:9; Deuteronomy 33:28)*

Speaking of Israel, the Bible has the following to say:

> *"...the people shall dwell alone, and shall not be reckoned among the nations." (Numbers 23:9)*

Israel is by purpose of existence unique, or one could even say, chosen, but chosen for what?

The seventy nations are Adam's natural decent and together they represent the full body of Adam, with nothing lacking. But, a body cannot live without a spirit to give it life, direction, and purpose. A lifeless body is but a corpse, and it is of no benefit to anyone.

Such was the case with Adam in Genesis 2:7. The dust of the earth was first formed into the being called man, but it was a lifeless shell on its own. So, God added something to the completed body, and that something was the breath of life, the spirit. It was the spirit which God bestowed unto Adam which made Adam alive and truly complete. Such is Israel's function in the earth: it is to be the life-giver and empowerer of the seventy nations by bringing to them the knowledge of the Living God.

Israel was created to be the life force of the body of Adam (the seventy nations). While the nations fully represent everything there is about Adam and they lack nothing, they cannot move, function, or properly activate their God given blessings without "life" first being given to the corporate body of man. Israel is created and sent to bring that life of God, that blessing of Messiah, unto the nations in order to give them life. The unique nation called Israel is "chosen" and created for that life giving purpose.

THE FAMILY

Now, when delving into the national way of governance, we will start with the first and most familiar level of governmental life, and that is the immediate family. This inherently close-knit group has direct blood and covenantal (marital) ties to one another and includes relations such as: dad, mom, children, grandparents, uncles and aunts, etc.

In the family structure there is a love-based order and organization, with each member of the family filling different roles. The younger pay homage to the elders through obedience, learning, and chores; and the elders in turn provide for and teach the younger the skills necessary to become successful members of their society. As is common with all things established by God giving of oneself is central to the makeup of the family construct.

THE CLAN

The second level of order is that of the clan, or the extended family. A clan is made up of numerous closely related families and individuals with either direct, or indirect, blood or covenantal ties to one another.

The kindred relations which exist between the families in a clan allow for a natural cohesion and symbiosis to flourish in their midst. With the clan construct providing immediate order, security, and stability within a community a basis for greater opportunities arise for each individual and family. The functioning clan allows for increased levels of safety, learning, networking, and even increased earning potential to come about for individuals, and a platform for increased personal charity is also achieved.

THE TRIBE

The third form of familial governance is that of the tribe. The tribal unit is made up of a number of clans and families, each having a form of a blood or covenantal relation to the other clans and families within the tribe, or they share certain links to a common distant ancestor.

The tribal contribution to God's design of governmental order is on a level naturally more distant from the individual, but it nonetheless holds important keys for a thriving life. The tribe provides individuals with a commonality of language, thought, and moral behavior in which to grow, learn, and eventually earn.

The tribe is responsible for external security and for the overall safety of its members, their possessions, and their land area. The tribe is the level of familial government responsible to raise armies in order to fight off any potential aggressor and to provide for the common defense of all its members. It is the tribal level which would see the raising up of judges from among its people for the establishment of law and order, guidance, and greater counsel.

In this level of family based government elders are also seen arising into positions of authority from which they can speak on behalf of all members in both internal and external matters of state. All of this is designed to promote the stability and cohesion of clans and families, which in turn can develop well rounded successful individuals who can arise to benefit society as a whole. It's a matter of all societal members giving of themselves which leads to a prosperous future for all concerned.

THE NATION

The fourth and final level of biblically instituted family based life government is the nation. This is, once again, a natural construct consisting of covenantal, kindred, and blood relations.

The nation is generally a tribe or a grouping of tribes sharing a common foundational heritage. That foundational heritage may consist of, but is not limited to: a common land, language, or religion. But, a nation, as originally defined in scripture, is always based upon a dominant common ancestry.

This common ancestry spoken of is an identification with one of the seventy progenitors mentioned in the biblical narrative in the tenth chapter of Genesis.

However, the nation is not defined by the modern artificial construct, the entity known as a "country", which is of an abstract hodgepodge origin at best. Nor is the nation necessarily limited to entities with political independence, or even to those which have a unified geographical existence. Unity and political independence are not prerequisites for a people to be biblically considered as a single nation.

A nation may, in fact, be composed of many disparate and far flung affiliates. Actually, there may be numerous tribal units or tribal allegiances from one nation which have wound up or chosen, for one reason or another, to live independently from one another; each composed of, and caring for, its own branch of the people, culture, land, language, and affairs of the nation.

These have become "peoples" within the nation and presently have independent futures, but they do not have independent original anointings. Such branched out and divided tribes are still linked together by the bloodline blessings of kin into one nation along with their slightly removed tribal relations.

Remember, biblically speaking there are only seventy nations upon the earth, and there can ONLY be seventy nations upon the earth. No amount of desertion or manipulation among the wayward children of Adam can alter that one evident truth.

JACOB'S TWINS

A biblical example of this permanent national unity is seen in the infamous tribal division of that most unique nation, Israel. *(1 Kings chapters 12-14; 2 Chronicles 10:1-11:4).*

When the northern tribes left the rule of the Davidic monarchy, they did not become a new nation with new anointings, blessings, and ethnic characteristics. They simply gave another new and different face to the nation of Israel, and the remaining Davidic monarchy of Judah was just as much Israelite as it had ever been, regardless of its different name.

Both countries had the same blessings, promises, and giftings which they were originally jointly blessed with, but the way in which they chose to live their separate political lives simply resulted in unique independent consequences for the two houses of that most unique nation.

THE DIVIDED CHEROKEE

Another example of these kindred blessings remaining with a divided people would be that of the Cherokee Indians of the southeastern United States. In the eighteen-hundreds, this tribe was forcibly moved by the federal government of the United States from its ancestral lands to territory in Oklahoma.

This forced resettlement caused a split between those Cherokee who were compulsorily marched from their homes in the southeastern United States into the territory of Oklahoma, and those who managed to avoid that fate and stay behind in the southeast. Both halves of the Cherokee people were still fully Cherokee, and carried the full characteristics of the people with them despite the physical separation and political divisions which occurred to divide them one from another.

NORDIC DESIGNS

Yet, a third example can be found in the Scandinavian countries. The majority ethnic peoples of Sweden, Norway, Denmark, and Iceland, while living in different independent "countries" today, all belong to the same nation. Their shared roots have established their commonality, and that fact well outweighs the manmade borders and different cultural nuances which have seeped in over the centuries to differentiate them from each other in this modern time.

"THICKER THAN WATER"

In other words, manmade political borders, actions, or events do not separate or exclude tribes, clans, or families of a nation from belonging to their own ethnic nation and partaking of that nation's God-endowed characteristics and blessings. The phrase "blood is thicker than water" is more true than we realize.

Outside of providing an ordered life, one of the main purposes of the nation is to ensure the continuity and safety of God's ethno-centrically bestowed Adamic blessings.

When God established the seventy nations and granted each of them their own particular blessings and characteristics, He did so with the full intent that those characteristics would perpetually continue in the earth along with each family group (nation) that carried them.

The nation is the strongest and best line of defense for the perpetuity of those familial bloodline blessings.

- An individual may move away from his or her people, may intermarry, or even die.
- A family may become dysfunctional or move away from its people, losing the conscious knowledge of its place in the world and its ability to properly shine that light of blessing forth.
- A clan may be driven to partition by a number of causes.
- A tribe may become assimilated into a strange or foreign culture and its way of life undermined by both time and events, and such actions may lessen its effectiveness at representing its unique Adamic aspects.

However, the nation will always remain in some state of existence to continue on and to ensure that the unique characteristics and blessings of Adam entrusted to it by God for safekeeping will remain upon the earth, with the potential always there for it to bless and strengthen the nations according to the design of God. That is the Creator's intent and promise, and it is love at work. *(Genesis 22:18, 26:4; Psalm 22:27; Revelation 15:4, 21:24-26)*

Family, clan, tribe, nation: In all four divisions of order, in all Godly levels of life government, the logic of love and kinship is readily evident; as is the individual's ability to preserve and grow that which God had kindly granted unto one's people.

The more an individual comes to appreciate the blessings upon his or her kindred the more that same individual is able to bring forth those granted blessings into the earth, and that, in turn, can come to bless the entire family of Adam.

INDIVIDUALISM

One type of government has not been touched upon in our look at the Godly way of life, and the absence of this form of rule has been purposed, for it does not have a rightful ruling place in God's design of life. That type of government is "individualism".

We have seen the importance of family, clan, tribe, and nation, but individualism has no value to add. On the contrary, it detracts from the richness of unity and plurality which the four levels of Godly design seek to bring about.

The Bible speaks about the erroneous path of individualism, and of its inability to genuinely profit mankind:

> "There is a way which seemeth right unto a man, but the end thereof [are] the ways of death." (Proverbs 14:12)

> "Every way of a man [is] right in his own eyes: but the LORD pondereth the hearts." (Proverbs 21:2)

The rule of individual will which fallen man has always considered to be central to existence is not presented as something conducive to life as defined by the biblical narrative. Individualism is focused on taking, and making oneself smarter, richer, and stronger in the eyes of others, greater than one otherwise would need to be. And, that leads, in its perverted way, to the root of empire.

THE EMPIRE

The second form of governance is called "empire". An empire is not a Godly design for life. It is, actually, a demonically designed construct used to dominate and destroy nations, tribes, clans, and families. This leaves the remaining element, the individual person, anchorless and manipulatable in a strange and foreign construct.

Empires are by definition, single political entities which rule diverse groups of nations, tribes, territories, or peoples for the benefit of a few individuals. Empires are antithetical to all ties of kinship and blood, for empires are designed to conquer, scatter, mix, assimilate, annihilate, bribe, or seduce any and all who fall into their ever expansionistic gaze.

That is the principal reason why the nation of Promise, Israel, is never referred to biblically as an empire. It simply cannot exist as an empire and remain able to fulfill God's will. And, Israel must be obedient to

The Empires of Image

God's design or its existence is pointless, and God's work in creating it is moot.

A look at the coming millennial reign of Messiah will show us that even during Israel's greatest time of rule, during the time of Israel's unquestionable authority in the things of man, it will still be a nation, a people (i.e. a family based ethnic group). Yes, it will be a preeminent and ruling nation, one with the final say in matters pertaining to life and Godliness, but it will be, nonetheless, a nation and a people among all others. *(Jeremiah 30; Ezekiel 37:22, 38:16)*

Israel, during the millennial reign, will not be an empire or a tyrant's home. It will be the nation of the Great King. And, all nations, tribes, clans, families.... and yes, even individuals upon the earth in that time will be given a free will choice. They can choose to align themselves with Israel and her King, or they can choose not to and live with the unenviable results.

Within God's plans free will is always respected, but in an empire free will and freedom are crushed. Even those individuals who are coerced into serving the empire do so under the control and rules of the empire which has first ground them into a malleable clump fit for the using.

These empires of which we speak were themselves at one time peoples or tribes to whose leadership individuals arose who were given to self-interest and greed. These fledgling tyrants inevitably sought to lead their misguided peoples into a life of control and power lust. The tribes in question soon found the perverted ways of plundering and politicking for conquest to be more lucrative than that of living their uniquely sanctioned lives in peace appeared to be.

However, as in all satanically contrived schemes, the specific peoples and tribes which become the seed corn of empire are themselves often the greatest victims of the demonic attack against the God ordered structure of life. For, in their pursuit of grandeur, their own identities and blessings inevitably become forfeit under the crushing weight of the self-imposed curse of empire.

These empires, spiritually conspired by satan and his ilk, are totally opposed to letting anyone live in peace or choose anything for themselves.

ENEMIES OF THE STATE

The war between empire and the national form of family based government has always seen the empire attacking the fourfold governmental system of God and freedom as it seeks to dominate all within its reach. The design of the family based system of existing is such a successful and powerful force, one devised to nurture and protect the individual, and in so doing, to reveal God's unique blessings upon all, that evil feels it a necessity to attempt the eradication of that Godly design.

Empires will always attempt to foist their wills and wants, their cultures and religions, upon all nations, tribes, clans, and families which they conquer irrespective of the desire of the conquered. These ungodly entities need to destroy the structure of the family based way of life, to stifle the free will and choice of nations and the creative individuals found therein, in order for their own deceptive illusions to survive.

Attacking and destroying the four levels of family based government brings about the rootlessness found in individuals who are then themselves ripe to be twisted into new perverse pawns of empire.

Now, when attempting to destroy the fourfold Godly design of life, multilevel attacks must be waged against each level of organization independently; for, *"a threefold cord is not quickly broken" (Ecclesiastes 4:12)*; nor is a fourfold structure of life. And so, empire must attempt to destroy the things it fears most, for those things stand in direct opposition to its very existence.

Here are a few ways in which the four levels of familial government have historically been attacked (this is not meant to be an exhaustive analysis, merely a brief topical synopsis):

FAMILY; TIES THAT BLIND

The family: The most important building block in life, the family offers protection, wisdom, and a sense of place like no other. The family is attacked and destroyed through the purposed enslavement of individuals in a variety of ways, both physical and spiritual. Countless families have been torn apart over the millennia by wars, death, enslavement, and outright poverty; much of which is instigated by empires upon the populace they seek to conquer or exploit.

On the spiritual side, an empirically instituted, governmentally initiated, lack of morality can, and has, cut the family unit to shreds countless times. Lawlessness, alcoholism, addictions, adultery, abuse, divorce, subsidized sloth, etc., and the general poverty of life which comes to the fore when the individual seeks to advance and please only self and foregoes the love of others, are the most common negative ways to destroy the family.

Aside from the previously mentioned negative assaults, another practical form of attack is based on a positive deception. That deception is prosperous individualism with an "anything goes" initiative which proudly touts the "me first" cry that leads to a false form of wealth. However, it also leads to a complete rout of all the essential building blocks of family inclusiveness, for the giving attitude is lost. And, once again, such an individualistic approach leads to rootlessness, displacement, and ultimately to a loss of the ever dear self-serving self.

CLAN CHOWDER

The clan: A structure extremely important for life, one which has upheld the citizens of the earth for dozens of centuries. The clan provides immediate order in life and allows its members a protective cover in which to live, work, and prosper. The simplest forms of attack on the clannish system are economic instability and societal destabilization.

Poverty and oppression, often enforced by the rise or onslaught of an empire, will drive the citizenry of one region to seek fiscal, social, or religious relief from other disparate and varied locales. This isolates the once unified clan members, leaving each one to fend for themselves in yet another organized enforcement of... individualism. In a rather short time, the ties of blood which have knit this structure together will have all but disappeared under the weight of the imperially devised individualist ideal.

"...GETTING AWAY "SCOT" FREE?"

An infamous example of purposed clan destruction is seen in the history of Scotland. The Scots were a clan based society which successfully faced and overcame numerous challenges: economic, climactic, military, and other. However, Scotland was located on the

The Nation Vs the Empire

same island as a burgeoning and ambitious seed corn of empire, England; the country which is at very heart of the British Empire. The powerful clan based society of Scotland withstood all challenges to its own way of life, but eventually succumbed to the much greater power of English imperial oppression.

Having unified the crown of the British isles under imperial British control in the 1600's, the enlarged English empire then outlawed the clans of Scotland altogether in the years following the 1746 A.D. battle of Culloden. The clans and their folk which served as security for the Scots and upheld the language and culture of the people for centuries were systematically discriminated against, oppressed, hunted down, and eventually decimated. This was done in order to rid the land of its existing familial order and to remove that competing force, which the empire deemed a threat, from its new "territory".

As long as the order and stability which the powerful clans gave unto the Scots remained, the British Empire couldn't fully control or manipulate the individual people or morph them into an image which best suited the goals of that particular empire. The stalwart proponents of the clans were eventually forced to leave the country, were imprisoned, or were killed and the remaining population was left rudderless and manipulatable, ready to be used in the service of the ever expanding... empire.

TRIB(E)ULATIONS

The tribe: Tying peoples of like heart together for millennia, the tribe stands as the unique voice of man's many family groups and clannish structures. This definite seal of identity is forged in the wealth of its clans and the wisdom of their people. The tribe is most often seduced into defeat by external (imperially instigated) thoughts and ideas, designed to either break or buy the tribal entity into eventual submission.

The many "native" tribes of the Americas, and those found within the boundaries of modern Russia, are perfect examples of tribal destruction by empires, not a few. With the tribal identity all but erased from the consciousness of many, a broken people emerges which has no past to cling to, no present to guide them, and no future for them to recognize.

In the wake of a vibrant and active tribal life emerges an alienation from one's own land and people, a sterile existence of perceived inferiority to the dominant imperial culture. A settling into all forms of poverty occurs for those not quite dead to the familial forms of government, and not quite accepting of the boorish empire. These routed peoples live days which are the scarred memories of so many souls.

It is commonly perceived that such people are "hanging on to yesterday and not embracing tomorrow". But, in reality, these people are rejecting the infringing rule of empire and its forceful implementation of will upon themselves in the only ways they know how. For, they still have a memory, however shattered and dissolved it may now be, which yet longs for the God given structure of the tribe, the clan, and the family, but none is to be found. Empire has had its way.

Lest the tribes of the Americas, or of "mother" Russia, are erroneously singled out in this saddening process, a reminder of tribal loss and misplaced identity can be found in all lands and upon all continents. Each person living today has had to deal with the loss of home and hearth brought to bear upon themselves and their bloodline by the pressing weight of empires in various forms. And, few things can be sadder than a life lived which has never known God's guiding will or intent for a people whose memory is all but lost.

All must choose to capitulate and yield to a bending before the great powers of the earth or resist them, and risk a breaking of crushing proportions coming upon themselves. Will the individuals of today cling to time honored truth or capitulate unto contrived convenience?

NATIONALS LAMPOONED

The nation: This great bulwark of blood ties, this protector of Adamic blessing, stands in constant conflict with empire. The nation is most often brought to its knees by wars, invasion, forced exile, and genocide. However, this is the one structure of the four which has its survival guaranteed by heaven's eternal design.

The nation may lose independence, it may see tribes split apart, clans torn apart, and families living apart, but the nation will always exist. No matter how tattered, hidden, or silent the nation may seem to be, God shall always see to it that each nation of the seventy will remain to be reawakened upon the repentance of its peoples in order to ensure that the Adamic blessings which each has been given shall come to the fore and play its unique part in the great orchestra of life.

Empires, as all evil constructs, designs, and schemes inevitably do, stand for blandness and impotent monotony. They are bereft of the vast flowering diversity of life found in the forests of nations for empires fell the rich woodlands naturally found, and leave a homogenous plantation crop of a harvestable timber called "lost souls" emerging in their stead. This implementation of controlled "growth for profit" souls creates a landscape that appears abundant in life, but it is little more than a desert seeded in pale green clones kept for the harvest.

The nations are not so, each was created to add a particular richness to the peoples of the earth and to allow Adam to bring forth in abundance upon the land. Each nation, with its own melody, was to add its unique sound into the beautiful "song of songs" conducted by the Creator Himself; with the myriad notes of the tribes, clans, families, and individuals within them all coming together into a harmony of life without compare. And, it shall yet be so, for come the millennial reign of the Anointed King Messiah the trees shall clap their hands and the mountains shall sing. *(Isaiah 55:12)*

But, as for now, yet doth the battle rage in the hearts of man...

CHAPTER TWO

STARTING OFF

"So God created man in his [own] image, in the image of God created he him..." (Genesis 1:27)

Back in the days of the beginning, when God first created man, He made Adam to be the perfect likeness of Himself in every way. Adam was literally created to be the living image of the Most High God upon this earth.

This earthen vessel called "man" (Adam) was granted dominion and rule over all things around him. Everything pertaining to this physical world was made subordinate unto him and he was well, living in the perfect garden which his Father, the Lord his God, had made. Peace and wellness reigned as long as Adam respected the will of God: but, then came man's foray into sin and the ensuing fall of Adam.

Due to the events which took place surrounding the well known, *"tree of the knowledge of good and evil" (Genesis chapter 3),* man found himself under the effects of the curse of sin and under the oppressive authorities of the wicked angelic conspirators (satan and his ilk), which operate through their inherited abilities in many aspects of the physical and spiritual worlds. *(2 Corinthians 4:4; Galatians 1:4)*

In the sequence of events which entailed the unlikely fall of man everything seemed to go upside-down in the creation. Adam (mankind), the God appointed ruler and protector of the physical domain actually became ruled by the physical world. Or, yet more pointedly, he became unduly bound and influenced by those transgressionary wicked angels within the creation who, at a time preceding their transgressions, had received God given authorities to oversee a great many things in God's heavens; including a great many things found within the physical world.

These authorities of supervision were first given out by God unto all of the angels, the yet to be wicked ones included, at a time long before wickedness first existed; at a time long before the satanic transgression first began. *(Job 38:7; Ephesians 3:10; Colossians 1:16)*

Since the Adamic fall, man, the intended and one time protector of all life in the physical creation, had, due to sin, become a huge detriment to that same life as he himself became an apparently willing vassal of evil, one which often sought to destroy and weaken all which God had established for good.

This unnatural, sinful, and perverted death loving nature which came to the fore of mankind's communal existence after the fall of Adam continued to flourish unabatedly from Adam's first bite of the forbidden fruit through unto the time of Noah's flood. Wickedness seemed to increase with the passage of time and with the arrival of each successive generation born into this sin stained world.

Conversely, righteousness continually decreased on the collective level as the number of people who loved God and sought righteousness lessened with every passing year eventually leaving Noah alone as the last of the righteous upon the earth. In that pre-flood time period man's thoughts were said to be: *"only evil continually" (Genesis 6: 5)*.

The unmitigated level of wickedness brought forth into the earth by the fallen family of a once holy mankind finally came to a close during the Noachian deluge which swept over and covered the surface of the entire earth. *(Genesis chapters 5-9)*

This cleansing event removed the near total unrepentant wickedness of man from upon the face of a sin ravaged creation. The being called man, created in the image of God, was all but removed from upon the earth in order for creation to regain any semblance of order. For man was corrupted and overshadowed by sin and insidiously used by the evil angelic conspirators to further their efforts of corrupting all facets of physical life in their attempts to defy the holiness of the Living God.

However, even the total removal of the unrepentantly wicked elements of mankind from upon the earth did not bring about the return of the lost Adamic freedom and dominion for the surviving remnant of Adam's Noahcic children. Mankind still languished, bound all but hopelessly, under the mighty curse of sin and under the dark influence of the utterly wicked angelic conspirators; albeit, not to the degree of near total willing co-operation in which Adam's children had previously existed.

AT 'IT' AGAIN

Before long, fallen Adam's post-flood children were at 'it' again ('it' being the promotion and exhibition of the depraved conduct which they were still enslaved to). A central part of that continued perversion was man's effort to form a wicked worldwide way of life; a communal existence for the rapid promotion and development of universal sin through the establishment of a system of complete global government centered in the city of Babel. The focal point of this Babylonian rule was a societal government which was formed in an effort to supplant the inalienable rights of God.

This first Babylonian government was established by man in an attempt to nullify and supersede the authority of God to involve Himself in the physical world of mankind, and to also enable mankind in its attempts to disregard the universal laws which God had created, and to do so in every possible way. These laws were designed by God in order to bring about life, blessings, and peace for all, but mankind would have none of it.

This establishing of a central human government in Babylon was an attempt to avoid God's will and rule by having the fallen and satanically subjugated family of man ostensibly rule itself. And, in so doing, spread any and all iniquities it chose to quickly and freely throughout its all too homogenous ranks. *(Genesis 11:1-9)*

Any success mankind would have had in stifling or limiting God's will and actions in, and among, the Adamic family and this physical world would have allowed mankind to act as it wished. Or, more precisely, to act as the wicked angelic conspirators would have had them to act.

Mankind would have then been able to freely enter into unbridled wickedness and evil, something which would have deprived the children of Adam of all remaining liberty and dignity. This would have inevitably caused all created life on the earth to be destroyed; as similarly happened in the days of Noah. *(Genesis chapter 6)*

This building of the Babel based government of man brought about the need for yet another God initiated intervention, namely, the scattering of peoples and the confounding of the tongues. This was established in order to keep the individually committed evils of the people separated from each other and thus weakened in overall effectiveness.

The Lord used this ingenious method of separation to protect the people of the earth from their own otherwise overwhelming collective sin. Such an action was an effective means for God to impose upon mankind a certain minimum degree of morality without unduly interfering with an individual person's previously granted right to free will and action. However, even these seemingly radical Godly measures did not free mankind from the self imposed yoke of evil first shouldered by Adam in Eden's green garden.

Mankind seemed permanently subjugated (often, all too willingly) unto the wicked principalities, powers, and rulers of darkness which held sway in this world, and nothing seemed to help change the hearts of man; not blessing or curse. For man was far and removed from God in both thought and deed. He was overshadowed by a heart of blackened stone and a mind swayed into corruption by the twisted satanic illusions found permeating the dust matter of the earth due to the presence of the wicked conspirators now entrenched in both their own substantial angelic authorities as well as in man's great, but Edenically subjected, authorities in the place once known as Adam's domain.

And, in that manner, things continued on in the darkness of the post tower of Babel upside-down world of the creation, with the scattered and separated children of Adam each living a far more isolated and austere individual existence of sin and separation from God than the previous generations had been subject to: All the while still fully bound by evil and all of its repulsive results.

God's original and eternal will for mankind seemed but a distant memory and a bygone dream of an age once past as mankind now lived in a "new reality", one which perversely saw life as primarily a lone physical existence of perverted self want and will.

THE CREATION OF THE NATION

Thankfully, things began to change in the generations following the dispersal of the nations from Babylon with the birth of the man called Abraham, the first Hebrew; the man who came to be known as "the friend of God". *(2 Chronicles 20:7; Isaiah 41:8; James 2:23)*

As faithful Abraham entered into covenant with the God of all creation and subsequently gave his yet to be born lineage unto that same God for care and protection, he, in so doing, allowed God to begin structuring a format which would eventually bring about the removal of the yoke of sin and satan from upon all of the children of Adam.

This covenant also allowed God to continue freeing creation from satan's twisted hold. Creation is on that God initiated journey out of darkness to this very day, and through the fulfilled promise of Messiah God's handiwork will soon behold its Liberty. *(Genesis 12:1-3; 1 Kings 9:5; Psalm 110:1; Hebrews 10:12-17)*

When this faithful fellow, Abraham, entered into covenant with God the Almighty shared with him certain things which would occur to his children in the future. These were to be events which Abraham's children needed to go through in order to bring themselves, mankind, and all of creation back into right standing with Him through their delivery of Eve's promised seed, the Messiah. *(Genesis 3:15)*

God informed Abraham that one of the pivotal events his children would experience was a long sojourn in a strange and foreign land. The Lord also informed Abraham that the inhabitants of this land would place his children into forced bondage. That strange land was Egypt, where Abraham's children, the nation of Israel, were to toil as slaves for an unyielding master. *(Genesis 15:1-16)*

The burdens they bore, and the punishments they received, during their long sojourn in slavery caused the children of Israel to cry out unto the God they barely knew for deliverance. They turned to the God of their fathers: the God of Abraham, Isaac, and Jacob for help. *(Exodus 2:23-24, 3:7)*

In the subsequent supernatural liberation of Israel from its tireless taskmaster, and through its national entry into eternal covenant with God through its acceptance of His commandments given during their stay at the foot of Mt Sinai, Israel became the sovereign nation of the Lord God of Hosts.

This fact carried with it enormous implications for the entire world, for as long as this supernaturally devised nation, Israel, stayed true to the Lord, His blessing would ensure that Israel would grow into a role befitting a people and a land which was God's.

This Israel, which had just previously been a nation of slaves, was destined to become the leading nation of the earth in every possible way, ruling without rival in the affairs of man. Israel was chosen and set to begin returning mankind back unto God and His will for man; thusly, Israel was set to begin restoring Adamic freedom and rule back unto the children of man by taking that same rule away from the wicked and power usurping angelic conspirators and their self-appointed terrestrial minions.

The wicked angelic conspirators which had sought to use fallen mankind to further defy God, and to corrupt and destroy the physical creation, and to eventually have mankind destroy itself were to find that the nation of Israel was God's specially selected weapon of war and His chosen instrument of vengeance upon them. Israel was groomed and selected by the Almighty to be the physical source for the ultimate destruction of all evil. *(Jeremiah 51:19-20; Deuteronomy 7:6-9)*

That leading and all inclusive position of power for the nation of Israel came to its historic territorial and political peak of existence during the reigns of Kings David and Solomon, who governed the nation in the years around 1000 B.C.

Now, despite the years of grandeur which were fleetingly achieved during the reigns of David and Solomon, Israel never actually entered into the full potential of its role as the heir of all things and as the conduit of all blessings upon the earth. It merely scratched the proverbial surface of its endless blessings, but the potential and intent of God was always there for Israel to become the sole worldwide power in every possible sense of the words.

In entering into its blessings, Israel would serve God by limiting, and ultimately ending, the might and effects of the principalities, powers, and rulers of darkness which sought to (and did) implement the tragic results of the Adamic curse upon all men.

Eventually, the rule of Israeli spiritual, cultural, and political might was to one day become uncontested in the earth according to the biblically instituted Word and will of God, for Israel was selected to be the vehicle of man's return unto righteousness. In other words, the earth has not yet seen the promise of God called the nation of Israel manifested in fullness as that fullness is hidden in the rein of Israel's Messiah. *(Isaiah 9:6-7)*

The God given right to the world pre-eminence of Israelite (Israelite since the giving of the law at Mt. Sinai was intended to be synonymous with God-ly) thought, culture, and spiritual might continued unabated despite the apparent failure of the populace to live up to God's scriptural intent; and despite the subsequent division of the land into two mutually antagonistic kingdoms in the era following the rules of Kings David and Solomon.

A HOUSE DIVIDED

The two separated and divided Israelite kingdoms were to be known as:

> 1. The Kingdom of Judah, which held the promises of rule, and contained within its borders the holy and eternal capital city of Jerusalem, and the Temple of the LORD. With it remained the Levitical and Aaronic priesthoods, and not least of all, the hereditary Kingship of Israel. *(Genesis 49:10)*

> 2. The Kingdom of Israel, which kept the national name, was made up of a majority of the tribes and populace of the nation, and held a greater part of the national territory.

This division of the nation which occurred during the reign of Rehoboam, the son of King Solomon, who ruled around the years 931-913 B.C. came as a direct result of the Words and covenants of God being disrespected by the nation's populace.

Although the two oddly divided Israelite nations of Judah and Israel were often engaged in hostility and open military conflict with each other, brought about by a fall into idolatry and general sin by both the leadership and populace of the divided nation of God, Israel as a collective whole was still the single "nation" unto whom the authority and promise of rule was granted. *(2 Samuel 7:24; 1 Chronicles 17:22; Ezekiel chapter 37)*

However, the right to inherit all things promised, and the ability to implement righteousness, was contingent upon Israel's willingness to follow God's Torah, his instruction. The more the nation would humble itself unto God's Word the more it would enter into, and exhibit, its inheritable rights. Conversely, the less Israel chose to obey, the less it would manifest the blessings of God and walk in its inheritance upon the earth.

Yet, despite its varying degrees of willing compliance to the God given instruction it received, or of its quasi-adherence to the covenants it had with the Lord, no other country could arise to overtake Israel as the nation with the foremost position of influence in human affairs which the House of Jacob was given. Such preeminence in the affairs of man was issued unto the sons of Jacob as an eternal gift from God, never to be removed.

Israel was destined to be the light of God shining in a world of darkness in fulfillment of the decrees of the Almighty and of the promises He, Himself, had made. The world and the mankind which God so loved was eternally sent this light called Israel, and whether that light chose to shine bright or not at any given time was irrelevant to the effectiveness of the eternal promises made.

Despite the warnings of the prophets, and the eventual judgments of God which brought about the weakened duopolistic state, the nation of Israel continued to willfully and stubbornly slide down the path of deliberate sin.

"...LEFT BY THE WAYSIDE"

Century after century, the nation refused to obey the commandments of God which it had agreed to abide by at Sinai. Even the greatest and most important commandment was left by the wayside (actually, it was the first to go) in Israel's long but unattainable quest to "be like the other nations". *(1 Samuel 8:20)*

This greatest commandment was found stated in Deuteronomy 6:5:

"And thou shalt love the LORD thy God with all thine heart, and with all thy soul, and with all thy might." (Deuteronomy 6:5)

The old yoke of sin, first taken up by man in the garden of Eden, was continually reapplying itself with force upon the bent and twisted backs of an enslaved mankind, even upon the backs of those who were in covenanted service to the Holy God. *(1 Kings 14:22-24; 2 Kings 16:2-4; Isaiah 57:3-10; Jeremiah chapter 3)*

THE COMING OF ASSYRIA

As such deep-rooted disregard for the covenants Israel had with God continued unabated in both houses of the divided nation an almost unfathomable thing happened; God allowed another nation to conquer and exile the inhabitants of the northern portion of the land of Israel. This banishment of the northern House wasn't merely an expulsion from the "land of promise"; it was a banishment from the very promise itself. The northern House of Israel was no longer able to stand in its role as God's redemptive vessel due to its headlong plunge into sin; therefore, God had to remove it from its place of prominence.

The nation that was found with the imperial goals necessary to arise and exile this backslidden daughter of God was Assyria. Assyria had received the necessary grant of permission from the Almighty to rise up and conquer the unconquerable; she was permitted to cast the northern tribes out of their inheritance and out of God's land.

Assyria was allowed to complete the end of the northern tribes' right to implement the will of God upon the earth through their ruling and reigning in His name and in His authority. Since those of the northern House of Israel scoffed at the honor and freedom of representing God, the northern House was to no longer have the ability to promote and cause God's will and Word to eventually live in the hearts and minds of Adam's children.

Assyria was more than happy to ensure that was so. This nation was specially selected by God to be His chosen instrument of judgment. It was brought forth to be a unique punisher of wayward nations and people. Assyria was a nation given to the art of pain. And, it came to serve God a little too well in this matter, for Assyria wasn't just any old nation; this was a nation given over to wholesale cruelty and destruction. It became a voluntary pawn of satan, one which delighted in destroying the nations of the earth. *(Isaiah 10:6-7)*

> *"Ah, Assyria, the rod of my anger; the staff in their hands is my fury! Against a godless nation I send him, and against the people of my wrath I command him, to take spoil and seize plunder, and to tread them down like the mire of the streets." (Isaiah 10:5-6)* ESV

God is never wasteful, and Israel's refusal to enter into its ordained place of rule caused God to protect the blessings which He had eternally granted unto the nation of Israel by allowing the sin-loving northern House to be removed from those blessings. This exiling and subjugation of the northern House was accomplished by Assyria in the year 722 B.C.

With the completion of the Assyrian invasion, and its occupation of the northern Kingdom of Israel, the long sojourn in a seemingly endless exile began for a great many of Abraham's promised seed... and, the world once again became that much darker.

> *"For the children of Israel walked in all the sins of Jeroboam which he did; they departed not from them; Until the LORD removed Israel out of his sight, as he had said by all his servants the prophets. So was Israel carried away out of their own land to Assyria unto this day." (2 Kings 17:22-23)*

This "casting aside" of Israel by God had many reasons and repercussions, but chiefly, it was done to protect those of the House of Israel, the children of His friend Abraham, God's own covenant nation who chose to stubbornly transgress against Him, from the full weight of His wrath.

Starting Off

That's right. The "casting aside" of Israel was not so much a "punishment", but rather a "merciful action" taken by God to allow Israel to avoid the terrible alternative which was the inevitable self-destruction of the sin soaked and unrepentant nation. Had the northern tribes continued to remain in the promise of God and in the Promised Land while blaspheming the promises of blessing in their sin loving, covenant breaking, state they would have had to endure the complete wages of their actions. *(Ezekiel 18:4, 18:20)*

"For the wages of sin [is] death..." (Romans 6:23)

But, God in His mercy cast the northern tribes out from before His face, allowing them to live under the shadows of the heathen nations in order that they could survive in His creation even though they had grievously sinned against Him and had broken the covenants they had with Him. The grace of God allowed the northern tribes to not be destroyed, but to instead live exiled, subordinate to the wills and ways of other nations, hidden away from the face of God under the coverings of the heathen for a long, but thankfully, for a limited time.

This "casting aside" and exiling which occurred enabled God to implement a legal and acceptable way for the northern House to exist in order that they might live to be returned home again one day to fulfill His will despite the overwhelming transgressions which they had committed against Him, and against the covenants they had with Him.

The fallible tribes of the northern House did not, and seemingly could not, keep covenant with God. But, God fully intended to keep and implement His covenant with them for the sake of their fathers: Abraham, Isaac, and Jacob, and for the sake of His own eternal Word which emphatically states that He will bless and keep Israel forever. *(Exodus, 32:13; 2 Samuel 7:24; Malachi 3:6)*

"...but as touching the election, [they are] beloved for the fathers' sakes." (Romans 11:28)

"...for thou hast magnified thy word above all thy name." (Psalm 138:2)

The Empires of Image

ENTER, BABYLON

Now, during the time of Israel's fall and exiling into Assyria, and in the years immediately pursuant, another nation was swiftly arising, but this was to be no ordinary nation. This was to be the first great spiritual empire of the earth. This was Babylon of the Chaldees, and because of her the world of man would change forever.

Approximately a century after it had conquered and exiled Israel, Assyria itself fell to the upstart and fast rising Babylonian empire in the years between 625 B.C. and 610 B.C. This fall of Assyria unto Babylon can be seen as a direct judgment of God upon the pretentious destroyer of the northern House of Israel. For although God gave Assyria the necessary permission and power to conquer Israel He did not sanction the brutal conduct of the invaders or their sin filled heathen ways.

Speaking of both the empowerment and sin of Assyria, God said the following through His prophet, Isaiah:

> *"Against a godless nation I send him, and against the people of my wrath I command him, to take spoil and seize plunder, and to tread them down like the mire of the streets. But he does not so intend, and his heart does not so think; but it is in his heart to destroy, and to cut off nations not a few;"(Isaiah 10:6-7)* ESV

Despite the severity of the exiling event, the banishment of the northern tribes of Israel was not the end of the northern House, which God emphatically promised to regather unto Himself in the Land of Promise in the end of days. Nor was it the end of Israeli dominance in the affairs of man in that time, for the southern Kingdom of Judah still remained sovereign; and Jerusalem stood within it.

The holy Temple rising at the heart of the city, and of the nation, attested to the fact that Israel remained the God ordained preeminent world force in thought and culture, if not in visible political might or territory. For as long as the Temple stood, God's presence was with the nation; accordingly, the remaining southern House still retained the authority to carry out His will. If only it would choose to do so.

Starting Off

However, the problem was that even the southern nation of Judah had chosen to transgress against the covenants of the Lord, willfully straying after the ways of the heathen. *(Jeremiah chapter 3, chapter 30, chapter 33; Hosea chapter 3; Kings 21:10-16; Jeremiah 32:20-35, 36:3)*

Judah had hardened itself to the point that it had no interest in being with God, or adhering to His ways. The people of Judah chose to deliberately live in sin regardless of the repercussions their actions had upon their own lives, or upon the kingdom of Judah itself, or upon the fallen family of Adam; which the nation of Israel was created to deliver. And, despite the defiling of the Word of God which took place as the Word was trodden asunder in Judah's headstrong desire to live as irresponsibly as it chose.

The fast rising Kingdom of Babylon having previously meted out punishment to, and then having usurped the power of its next-door rival, Assyria, replaced it as the new overlord of the Middle East. This power starved up-and-comer, Babylon, was to then set its sights upon the remaining Hebrew Kingdom of Judah, which yet stood. This it did in its drive to spread itself, and its will, across the face of the earth. Its attempts to conquer Judah would have been for naught except for one important detail; Judah kept on tenaciously sinning against God, ever darkening her communal heart with all manner of defilement and wickedness.

Judah refused to learn from the tragic events which befell her sister to the north. The nation and the people continued to steadfastly sin and transgress against God and His Word despite Israel's complete collapse and banishment, and despite the tireless calls from the prophets of God for the nation to repent. *(Jeremiah 29:19)*

The southern Kingdom seemed stubbornly headed toward the same fate which befell the northern tribes. But, was it to be the same fate?

The answer is: No.

Judah's exile would prove to be exceedingly different from that of her sister's, and it would come to cost mankind a great deal more than anyone could have thought or imagined: For in its exile, Judah was also removed from her right to bring the rule of God's blessings into the affairs of man.

This meant that the children of Adam were to lose the one force which was designed and destined to bring forth righteousness into the world. The one power which could have eventually implemented the will of God upon the earth through its unique service to God had lost its authority to do so. The authority still existed, as it eternally would, as all Godly decrees inevitably do; but the right of Judah to access that authority and fully implement it was to be lost in the exile.

When God granted Babylon the right to banish Judah from His land the world would change forever. For the crown had been removed from the nation of kings (Israel) just as the nation had previously chosen to remove itself from the crown (God and His Torah). That crown would not be returned unto Israel again until Messiah will be anointed King and the nation through Him is reconciled unto God.

At that time, Israel, through the King Messiah, would be able to finally enter into its full role as the nation and land of Promise and bring all nations through itself into the will of God. However, until that time, the world awaits in darkness. *(Ezekiel chapter 36; Psalm 130; Revelation 12:5, 19:15)*

The ever expansive empire of Babylon was more than eager to accept the task of removing Judah from its rightful place as the head of nations, and it salivated at the prospect of destroying the Temple of the Most High, leaving the promise of worldwide redemption smoldering in the ruins of a once Holy place as Babylon pressed its scarring stamp of dominance onto the bowed backs of an already fallen mankind.

By the year 586 B.C., the independent Hebrew nation became little more than a relic of the past. It was reduced to being a "hidden entity", existing only in shadows and behind the scenes of history, as it flowed under the surface of both time and exilic tide. *(Deuteronomy 4:27, 28:64-65, 30:1)*

As was the case with the northern House of Israel, this banishment was God's over abundant mercy at work. God was hiding Judah from His full wrath and justice under the covering shadows of the heathen nations until the time of allotted punishment is past. *(Hosea 6:1-2; Deuteronomy 4:27-31; Ezekiel chapter 30; Jeremiah 51:5)*

Starting Off

The nation of Israel was not to be seen again as a sovereign state for some 2500 years, and in Israel's loss of rule (both kingly and priestly) all the nations of the earth were plunged into a spiritual darkness which is still felt to this day. Babylon of the heathen was given charge over the course of mankind, and a man named Nebuchadnezzar was decreed to be its king. *(Jeremiah 28:14)*

CHAPTER THREE

BEHOLD, THE DREAMER!

THE KING'S DREAMY DILEMMA

As Babylon entered the vacuum of power created by the sin and negligence of Israel's two divided kingdoms it successfully conquered the remaining Kingdom of Judah and destroyed the Holy Temple. As it did, it exiled the inhabitants of the land from the once great promise of God and left a taste of the wages of sin in its destructive wake.

Having done so, Babylon sought out from Judah the best and the brightest of its then captive youth to serve the Babylonian king in his expansive empire. Among those bright Jewish youths was a God fearing lad named Daniel, who quickly gained favor among the Babylonian ruling elite for his intelligence and understanding in matters both spiritual and natural.

Over the course of time this Jewish lad, Daniel, became one of the most respected counselors of the Babylonian king, Nebuchadnezzar. Daniel would also be instrumental as God's mouthpiece to the king and to all men unto this very day, for while in the exile Daniel became a great prophet of the Most High God.

In the second year of Nebuchadnezzar's reign over his vast empire a dream was given unto him by God, and not surprisingly, that dream troubled him exceedingly. This spiritual dream was to give the king insight into things far beyond his natural scope of knowledge. It was

The Empires of Image

going to explain the state of the world and its future to Nebuchadnezzar, and consequently, through him unto all who would hearken unto the Word of God.

There was a problem however, Nebuchadnezzar couldn't remember the dream! He knew that he saw it; he knew that it was an important dream, a spiritual dream, but he couldn't remember what it was. So, he did what only a tyrannical king could do after exhausting all logical options; he tried to force the dream and its explanation from the mouths of his counselors by using the most extreme measures available to him.

Needless to say, positive results were not forthcoming. That is, until Daniel was made aware of the king's demands and of the counselors' grim plight; they were all destined to be killed if they didn't solve the king's dreamy dilemma.

Daniel and his three fellow Jewish compatriots immediately set into prayer and supplication unto the God of Israel seeking the answer to that most vexing issue of nocturnal slumber. The faithful God of their fathers answered Daniel and his friends by giving them full knowledge of the dream and of its interpretation. Daniel was thusly able to convey the dream and its amazing meaning unto the king. He thereby fulfilled the will of God concerning the revelation of the issue, and he was also able to save the lives of the king's doomed counselors in the process.

A portion of Daniel's reply to the king is found following:

> *"Thou, O king, sawest, and behold a great image. This great image, whose brightness [was] excellent, stood before thee; and the form thereof [was] terrible. This image's head [was] of fine gold, his breast and his arms of silver, his belly and his thighs of brass, His legs of iron, his feet part of iron and part of clay. Thou sawest till that a stone was cut out without hands, which smote the image upon his feet [that were] of iron and clay, and brake them to pieces. Then was the iron, the clay, the brass, the silver, and the gold, broken to pieces together, and became like the chaff of the summer threshingfloors; and the wind carried them away, that no place was found for them: and the stone that smote the image became a great mountain, and filled the whole earth. This [is]*

the dream; and we will tell the interpretation thereof before the king."(Daniel 2:31-36)

Daniel revealed the dream and then he went on to give the amazing explanation of its meaning to the king. Daniel informed the king that the golden head of the statue was the king and his kingdom of Babylon, and that each of the statue's other body sections formed of the various different materials were other, later, kingdoms to come.

"Thou, O king, [art] a king of kings: for the God of heaven hath given thee a kingdom, power, and strength, and glory. And wheresoever the children of men dwell, the beasts of the field and the fowls of the heaven hath he given into thine hand, and hath made thee ruler over them all. Thou [art] this head of gold. And after thee shall arise another kingdom inferior to thee, and another third kingdom of brass, which shall bear rule over all the earth. And the fourth kingdom shall be strong as iron: forasmuch as iron breaketh in pieces and subdueth all [things]: and as iron that breaketh all these, shall it break in pieces and bruise. And whereas thou sawest the feet and toes, part of potters' clay, and part of iron, the kingdom shall be divided; but there shall be in it of the strength of the iron, forasmuch as thou sawest the iron mixed with miry clay. And [as] the toes of the feet [were] part of iron, and part of clay, [so] the kingdom shall be partly strong, and partly broken. And whereas thou sawest iron mixed with miry clay, they shall mingle themselves with the seed of men: but they shall not cleave one to another, even as iron is not mixed with clay. And in the days of these kings shall the God of heaven set up a kingdom, which shall never be destroyed: and the kingdom shall not be left to other people, [but] it shall break in pieces and consume all these kingdoms, and it shall stand for ever. Forasmuch as thou sawest that the stone was cut out of the mountain without hands, and that it brake in pieces the iron, the brass, the clay, the silver, and the gold; the great God hath made known to the king what shall come to pass hereafter: and the dream [is] certain, and the interpretation thereof sure. (Daniel 2:37-45)

INTERPRETERS ANONYMOUS

Throughout the ages, many Bible scholars, both Jewish and Christian, have understood the different body sections of this statue of empire to be properly interpreted (more or less) in the following way:

- The golden head was unquestionably Babylon according to scripture.
- The arms and breast of silver was Media-Persia.
- The belly and thighs of brass were Greece.
- The legs of iron were Rome.
- Finally, the feet, made of iron mixed with miry clay; that is the fifth unnamed kingdom yet to come.

This statue, made in the image of a man formed from these various different metal parts, would be destroyed once Messiah comes to establish His Kingdom; the kingdom of the stone, *"cut out of the mountain without hands"*.

The reasoning behind this commonly accepted interpretation of scripture is quite sound and logical as we shall soon discover. However, there is one specific reason why this explanation should be considered accurate, a reason so overwhelmingly compelling that it cannot be ignored, and that reason is: Whenever a large number of both Jewish and Christian scholars agree on *anything* it stands to reason they might be on to something. It's such a rare occurrence!

NAMING NAMES

A few of the names of famous historical biblical scholars among both Jews and Christians/Catholics who held this common understanding of the statue of Nebuchadnezzar's dream are as follows:

Among Jews: Rashi, Abraham ben Meir Ibn Ezra, Japet Ibn Ali, and Saadia ben Joseph haGaon.

Among Christians/Catholics: Martin Luther, Hippolytus, Augustine of Hippo, and Thomas Aquinas.

Alright, we've had enough ecumenical name dropping, for now. Next, we'll briefly look at some of the thoughts behind the reasons each previously mentioned kingdom should be understood to belong in the statue and hold its particular place therein. We'll start with the golden head of Babylon and move down the length of the statue.

BABYLON

The Bible itself in Daniel 2:38-39 says that the golden head of the image was Babylon. So there can be no question about its placement or position in the statue; not even the grumpiest of theologians can find much reason to quarrel about that!

MEDIA-PERSIA

The reasons to believe that the silver arms and breast were the empire of Media-Persia are as follows:

1. Persia plays an unusually prominent and important part in the biblical narrative, one that sees its active involvement in the earth's happenings through unto the end of days. Only a nation with such an important role could find its way into the statue of rule.

2. Media-Persia conquered the previously ruling empire, Babylon, and consequently "inherited" the dominant position in the world.

3. This Persian Empire and the authority of its king, while unusually great, wasn't as all encompassing in power and might as the Babylonian was during its reign. So its worth, while extremely high, was considerably less than that of the Babylonian gold. It was pictured as valuable silver compared to precious gold.

4. The position as the arms and breast in the statue fit this dual kingdom of Media-Persia perfectly. For this statue, a replica of a man, if it was to be true to its image would have had a dominant arm; it would have been either right handed or left handed, and the favored arm would have been the stronger.

That was exactly the case with Media-Persia. The Persian part of this dual kingdom was unquestionably the dominant and stronger of the two. Media was the "tag along" partner of this dynamic duo, so to speak.

Media was strong, but it was definitely a lesser associate in the combined kingdom. So, in Media-Persia, we see the historically rare political construct of a "dual kingdom" represented in the two arms of the statue reflected in a surprising perfection.

This fact of a dual kingdom with one of the nations holding a dominant position can also be clearly seen in a reading of the eighth chapter of Daniel. The empire of Media-Persia is pictured in this chapter as a ram with two horns, and one of the horns, the one that came up later, was larger than the other. And again, Persia chronologically rose to power after Media, and it was stronger than Media in all ways; it was the larger horn. There just aren't any other nations that can fit the prophetic silver setting in the statue in so many ways and as well as Media-Persia can.

> "Then I lifted up mine eyes, and saw, and, behold, there stood before the river a ram which had [two] horns: and the [two] horns [were] high; but one [was] higher than the other, and the higher came up last." (Daniel 8:3)

> "The ram which thou sawest having [two] horns [are] the kings of Media and Persia." (Daniel 8:20)

And finally, the words of Cyrus, the king of Persia, stand as a very strong testament of scripture confirming Persia's place of rule:

> "...the LORD stirred up the spirit of Cyrus king of Persia, that he made a proclamation throughout all his kingdom, and [put it] also in writing, saying, Thus saith Cyrus king of Persia, The LORD God of heaven hath given me all the kingdoms of the earth; and he hath charged me to build him an house at Jerusalem..." (Ezra 1:1-2)

GREECE

The next part of the statue is the belly and thighs of brass understood to be Greece.

The first reason why Greece is said to hold this position in the image is quite straightforward and simple. Greece had conquered Persia which had previously conquered Babylon. In so doing, Greece came into the unique right to govern the earth which was previously held by Persia and before it by Babylon, the original usurper of power after Israel's and Judah's exile.

A simple reading of Daniel chapter eight would clearly show the Grecian empire setting its sights on Media-Persia and then enthusiastically thrashing it and toppling it. *(Daniel 8:5-25)*

Second, being without a stable long lasting dynasty or a large "home" country the Greek empire was not "precious" in power as was silver Persia, and golden Babylon. Hence, it was symbolized by a strong and useful, definitely functional, but unmistakably non-precious alloy, brass. This metal alloy is once again an unusually good analogy for the multi-ethnic Greek empire which united together in strength under its powerful kings.

Third, Greek thought and culture was to sweep over the known world in an unprecedented fashion leaving its indelible stamp on all things. Only a nation which was enabled by God could have such far reaching power and success in spreading its ways into every field of human endeavor. All aspects of nearly every society, both modern and ancient, are influenced to some degree by Greek knowledge and customs.

Even the Bible itself is not without a Greek connection. Greek influence on both the "Old Testament" and "New Testament" is evident with the Bible's pages brimming with references to Greece in prophecy, as well as being replete with Greek and Grecian cultural and linguistic influences. Greece has been, and remains, a worldwide cultural power second to none and most fittingly holds its place as the very belly of the metallic beast.

ROME

Now for the legs of the statue, these are said to be the Roman Empire. Why? Well, first of all, over the course of time Rome, conquered the fragmented remains of the Greek empire piecemeal and that conquering was to be inclusive of the very heartland of Greece itself.

Thus, Rome came to inherit the rulership of the world from Greece, which had taken it from Persia, which had previously usurped it from Babylon, which came by it through divided Israel's infamous fall. The established right to dominate the world was only held by one nation at a time and could only be transferred to one other nation in an organized succession of "inherited" power.

This gentile and pagan control of the world wasn't biblically prophesied to be a divisible right which was held by numerous physical nations simultaneously. Therefore, this right to rule was limited by both Godly decree and numeric logic to move down the line of succession in clear steps of progression. Or, one can more accurately say, in clear steps of deterioration: from gold to silver, from silver to brass, and from brass to iron. Rome had clearly inherited the right to rule from the previous holders of that authority giving it a fitting place in the statue, one that only it could fill.

Next, the fact that its position would be seen as the two individual legs of the image is very appropriate and it fits Rome well, for Rome was also to be a divided empire. The successful division of an empire such as Rome into two independent and yet fully functional halves would be an event rarely witnessed in the history of the world.

With Rome split into western (Roman) and eastern (Byzantine) halves in the year 285 A.D. its culture and values, rather than receding due to divisional weakness, were able to carry on far beyond its years. Each half worked to uphold the concepts of Rome and propel its version of Roman culture into times and nations far beyond its respective borders. The fact that peace endured, as markedly as it did, between these neighboring "super twins" gives us a glimpse at their unusual divided state of unity.

The two halves of Rome would serve to control their separate dominions in an intellectually and politically symbiotic arrangement of power seldom achieved upon the earth. It was almost as if they were the right and left legs of the same entity, and indeed, the dream of Nebuchadnezzar shows us that is exactly what they were.

Finally, it is also most fitting for Rome to stand as the legs since they were made of iron. Iron is a common metal, and Rome had neither the all-powerful royal dynasties with unquestionable authority over their territory, nor did it have the absolute and dominant rule of the "world" which the other more precious empires that came before it did. However, Rome was as tough as iron in all things and it was not afraid to wield that strength against those who were seen as its rivals, whether political, geographical, or religious.

Now, as unbelievable as it may seem, when it comes to the things of man, the empire of Rome, though it is political and geographic history today, still holds the reigns of the world. For that fact to change, another organized empire, the fifth empire of iron and clay must rise to conquer and claim the vestiges of the once great physical empire of Rome. Only after the fifth empire has done so can it 'inherit" the right to rule as the preeminent empire upon the earth.

Time is immaterial in this matter, the destruction of Rome by implosion or marauder is irrelevant as well. The only thing that can unseat Rome from its present position of imperial power in the world of man is another physical empire.

Therefore Rome, however bruised, beaten, or sullied it may superficially now appear to be, and however silent it has been over the course of the centuries as a political force, is still at the helm of the satanic ship sailing across the seas of a fallen and bruised mankind.

One look at the world around us indicates that the conquering Rome is still very much with us today:

The political systems of most nations are greatly influenced by the Roman models of government. The militaries of present day nations owe a great debt to the Roman war machine which taught the world discipline, efficiency, and battle tactics like no other. The engineering and architectural marvels of the earth rise from a Roman foundation. The language of medicine, law, and western religion is, to a great degree, the language of Rome, which is Latin.

Indeed, the religious roots of most people in the Christian and, arguably, in the Islamic world today stem from the twisted branches of a Roman tree.

Why, even the alphabet used when there are large international gatherings or sporting events taking place, such as the Olympic Games, etc., is almost exclusively the Roman alphabet; not the Cyrillic, Arabic, Hebrew, Chinese, Japanese or Korean alphabets, but the Roman alphabet.

It is still a Roman world today. That world, held by Rome, is what the empire of iron and clay will come to conquer and inherit.

THE FIFTH EMPIRE

As for the feet of the statue, those of mixed iron and clay, their time is yet to come. That empire will rise to become the inheritor and usurper of Rome's might as well as of the global right to rule which was held by Rome and inherited from the other previously empowered empires.

The questions may well be asked: If Rome is ancient history how can another empire rise to inherit its right to rule? Wouldn't the approximately 1500 year time gap between the two empires make conquering and inheriting the power of a defunct Roman empire either useless or downright impossible?

The key to understanding these issues comes in realizing that all of the preceding empires had their right to rule not only in the political sphere, but more importantly, in all aspects of mankind's existence as affected by the physical world.

As each successive empire inherited the dominant position of power in the world from the previous it did so in all aspects of life affecting man's physical tenure upon the earth, not only politically or geographically. That overriding power which these empires each held was eventually inherited by a conquering Rome, but Rome itself was never conquered by another empire. It imploded, it was sacked, weakened, invaded, and besieged by various foreign tribes and nations over the course of time; it was torn apart piecemeal, but it was never conquered by another empire. Therefore, despite its apparent physical and geographic weakness, Rome, from the spiritual standpoint of empire, still stands today and it does so as the dominant power in the affairs of man.

The curious thing about the fifth empire to come is that it is partially of the same material as the Roman legs were, for it is iron that is mixed with clay. This means that it will be quite similar to Rome in all things, similar, but due to its miry clay content it is not the same.

This final gentile kingdom may even appear to be ostensibly Roman in all things, but it will be quite different in that it will have an element of division and separation in it which Rome and the other previous ruling empires did not have. It is this fifth power that will enthusiastically take possession of the right to rule from the great empire which it will eventually come to topple.

Another interesting fact to note about the makeup of the fifth empire is that the clay in the feet of the statue is the only non-metallic element mentioned in any of the layers of the image.

What are the characteristics of clay?

Clay is common; it is weak, and it has little value of its own. When used in pottery it is vulnerable to damage; it simply doesn't hold together as firmly as a metal would, nor does it bond solidly to any other materials such as to metal or to wood.

Notably, clay is actually much closer in elemental composition to the stone which will come to shatter the statue than it is to any metal. The vast difference being that clay is a fine grained silty substance; it is essentially eroded pulverized rock held together by pressure, moisture, or baking, whereas a stone is one solid piece of uneroded rock which hasn't been worn down by the elements of decay found in the natural world.

Our Messiah Yeshua (Jesus) is that stone; that uneroded Rock. Nothing of this world was able to wear Him down into clay!

> "[He is] the Rock, his work [is] perfect: for all his ways [are] judgment: a God of truth and without iniquity, just and right [is] he." (Deuteronomy 32:4)

What does the clay represent in this statue?

Its presence speaks of the inherent divisions of the peoples found in the fifth empire and of their inability to unite in strength. It may also be a way for God to reveal unto us the nature of the fallen and perverted ways of man active within the statue.

For mankind was originally made into the image of God (the Mountain), and of Messiah (the stone cut out of the mountain), and individuals of the fallen family of man could well be understood to be represented by the individual clay particles, the silt or crushed eroded rock, which have been unnaturally reassembled and brought together as clay, and as pieces of podiatric pottery.

In this case, the clay (the entire fallen family of man) is mixed into the final fifth part of the cast statue. This shows us mankind's part in the wicked end time endeavor to bring about a result on the earth which is other than the will of God.

The clay may well be showing us another attempt at a tower of Babel type system of false unity, one which again attempts to have man usurp the authority of the laws of God, but instead brings about a great division in the ranks of its own rule.

Possibly, the presence of the clay in the feet of the statue may refer to a manmade system, perhaps religious, exerting itself in the fifth empire, one which is antithetical to the truth of God and of the rock to come (the Messiah).

The clay and iron mixture indicates that this empire will not be cohesive or united in any tangible way, but nevertheless it will have great power and it will possess the same characteristics as those of iron Rome, the same which are dominant in our world today. *(Daniel 2:43)*

The clay, which is finely ground stone, could also be seen as a perverted form of God's original intent for mankind, which was for man (Adam) to be a stone cut from the mountain, which is God. That is, for man to be the image of God rather than to be destructively ground and crushed into the miry silt of clay (as mankind now is) by the wicked angelic conspirators which seek to inhibit God's will and destroy His creation.

Clay, which is stone crushed into fine silty powder, is what man has become as a result of the curse of sin implementing its power upon the family of fallen Adam, who was the original stone of God, (the first chip off of the Block as it were). This is also similar to how the last Adam, Messiah, is spoken of as the coming stone in the second chapter of Daniel.

In the silt particles that are brought together and formed into the clumps of clay revealed in this image of wickedness we can see the evil conspirators molding and shaping the mankind which they have first weakened and crushed into powder, reshaping mankind into something seemingly beneficial to their interests.

As pictured here, fallen mankind has been crushed by evil and then reconstituted by the satanic transgressors, clumped together and molded into their will as clay would be, then put to wicked use in order to uphold and bring about the will of the wicked conspiracy upon the earth. This will be especially evident during the time of the fifth empire to come.

CHAPTER FOUR

ANOTHER LOOK

In the previous chapter we have seen the most common form of interpretational understanding used for explaining the different parts of the statue revealed to us in Nebuchadnezzar's dream. Now we will look at what else the statue can tell us. And, in order for us to receive a deeper understanding of this image found in the king's dream we must remember that before this "gentile" statue rose to its place of power in the earth the nation of Israel had been given the right, blessing, and obligation to lead the peoples of the earth and to serve as their priests, prophets, and kings.

It was to be Israel's God given role and destiny to be the greatest and most overwhelming influence in the lives of all men everywhere; in every possible way. In all facets of life Israel was to be a positive and holy influence guiding the people of the earth ever closer to the Lord God and His will.

Israel was formed to be a beacon, a light unto the nations, and an advancing bulwark of holiness raised against the oppression of satan and the influence of the curse upon mankind.

Not only was Israel to guide men towards righteousness, but as God's representative it was to exert a great degree of direction in the spiritual lives of all men. In that way, Israel would deliver and keep them from the terrible bondage of the fall induced oppression of evil.

The Empires of Image

It was precisely with the removal of Israel from its place of dominance in the world of man, evidenced by the destruction of the holy Temple of God in Jerusalem, that this beast of a statue was able to surface and come into the fore of human existence to further deny mankind access to the truth of God.

In other words, the reign of the statue of empire was to be an antithetical counterpart to the reign God intended Israel to have.

Where Israel was to shine forth the very radiance of God's life and love, the empires of this sordid image sought to bring a shadow of smothering death. Where Israel was to bring light, the empires of the image brought darkness. Where Israel was to promote holiness, the empires advanced evil and depravity, etc. etc.

Furthermore, in order to properly comprehend the magnitude of this image whose, *"form thereof was terrible"*, we must gain an understanding of the angelic host and of their workings. The angelic are deeply entwined with this dream and its prophesy just as they are active throughout the entire Book of Daniel and present within the whole creation narrative of the Bible.

Each created angel was blessed of God with certain anointings, abilities, and authorities with which they could serve God in the upkeep and care of His creation. In fact, everything in the creation is managed and cared for by the angelic host with each individual issue or thing in creation under the charge of a specific angel. *(Psalm 91:11, 103:20)*

This bestowal of authority would also include the care and oversight of the individual nations of the world, their provinces, and the cities found within them. Each specific nation and political area has its own angelic prince, power, or ruler to guide it along and defend its rights to exist, grow, and "prosper".

That angel would also stand before the heavenly court against any challengers or threats to the nation or region arising from other sources such as another political force for example, and plead his case before God. *(Daniel 10:13, 10: 20-21, 12:1)*

These great seats of power and blessings were issued unto the angels long before any of the angelic host actually transgressed and turned against the Lord, and the now evil angels were therefore also included in the issuance of these great blessings of God. Thus, the wicked found their way into the affairs of the earth.

Actually, anyone who does a close study of the Bible, and of the angels found therein, will be hard pressed to find any political principality, power, or ruler which is not transgressive and wicked. That is, other than Israel's angel prince, the archangel Michael, who faithfully stands with God.

According to the biblical narrative Michael is the only one of the angels in the political arena that is not wicked and conspiratorial; the others all seem to be evil. That includes the angel princes of the nations-turned-empires found in the statue of Nebuchadnezzar's dream.

In light of these two previously mentioned facts, of Israel losing its right to rule in the affairs of man, and of that right being given to certain gentile powers, each with wicked angelic princes overseeing their development and function, we are able to begin receiving an understanding of why Daniel described the form of the statue as, *"terrible."* For in the existence and prominence of this statue of empires upon the earth, with each empire therein inspired and guided by a wicked angelic prince, the fallen family of mankind was shown to be subjugated unto a wicked world order not of God's making.

Daniel came to understand from this dream and its explanation that the life which fallen mankind considered to be normal upon the earth was anything but. The chief perpetrators of the lie called "normal everyday life" were exposed in this troubling night image with the history and future of fallen mankind explained both on a communal as well as on an individual level. And, that story is one which affects each and every person on the planet.

THE GRAVITY OF THE SITUATION

To help us comprehend the gravity of these events and issues let's once more look at what it means when it is said that Israel was given the right to rule in the earth and to reign in the affairs of man. That right was to influence the soul and spirit of the individual person as well as to affect the entire political/physical function of individuals and nations.

The right to rule was to be over and affect all aspects of mankind's life in a positive way. This fact is best pictured in the coming millennial Messianic era when the King of the Jews shall arrive to re-establish the fallen booth of David and rule all things and people in righteousness through His regathered Kingdom of Israel. Through Israel, and its dominant reign in the future Messianic age, the evil inclination which now unnaturally exists in the hearts of natural men and attempts to lead them to doom and destruction will be vanquished and replaced by a will to prefer righteousness, peace, and holiness over evil and death.

In that time, when the will of God for the nation of Israel shall finally come to fruition, all men, even the non-repentant of every nation, will be inclined to prefer good over evil. This they will do without great effort or exertion for they will be naturally inclined to value all life over death as the yoke of wickedness will have been removed from man in the return of all power unto Israel and its King.

Before that time can come into effect, however, the empires of Nebuchadnezzar's statue, those which came to the forefront of power due to Israel's demise, will have to be thoroughly destroyed.

Remember, there can only be one nation at a time ruling atop the throne of man, and when God returns the power of rule unto Israel through Messiah the right of rule held by the heathen empires will be gone along with the satanically inspired empires themselves. This means that the world which the satanic conspirators fabricated to deceive and imprison mankind with will no longer exist. *(Colossians 2:15)*

The life promoting and blessed type of existence which God originally provided for mankind, and which He will re-implement through Israel's return from the exile, will be quite unlike the present corrupt existence, thought process, and culture which exist and are so prevalent in the world today where people seem to illogically thrive on the hurt of others, and seek to take every advantage over their peers in their quest to live in order to please only themselves.

Mankind today lives in a time period when the nation of Israel has backslidden and has been exiled from its promise and role for a season of time, and the heathen nations with their long established evil angelic leadership have been granted the control of man's world.

This age is known as the, "time(s) of the gentiles", and it has left mankind in a state where darkness ever presses into the fore of man's personal and communal way of life to implement the curse of the Adamic fall upon all. Nebuchadnezzar's statue will come to show us what this actually means, and how Israel's loss of rule has come to impact every person in existence.

A NEBUCHADNEZZARIAN WAKE UP CALL

AKA

"YOU SNOOZE... YOU LOSE"

But, first of all, what proof do we have that the defeat of the Jewish nation, the exile of the people, and the destruction of the holy Temple was a pivotal event both in scripture and in mankind's history; an event great enough to have begun a period considered a new and darkened age known as the, "time(s) of the gentiles"?

Let's turn back to scripture for the answer:

> "And in the second year of the reign of Nebuchadnezzar Nebuchadnezzar dreamed dreams, wherewith his spirit was troubled, and his sleep brake from him." (Daniel 2:1)

This one verse, and the second chapter as a whole, make the point implicitly. For according to the scriptural narrative Nebuchadnezzar had reined as the king of Babylon for many years prior to this notable night of troubled sleep and not just for the two years mentioned here; and he had specifically warred against Judah for many of those previously mentioned years. Yet, this verse clearly states that the dream(s) took place, *"in the second year of the reign of Nebuchadnezzar"*.

What's going on?

If the dream had taken place during the second year of Nebuchadnezzar merely ruling as the king of Babylon he would not have had the time to besiege and conquer Judah, or destroy the Temple, or commit all of the deeds the other biblical accounts speak of when mentioning Nebuchadnezzar's actions which took place prior to this night.

For example, if this dream actually took place in his second year of reining as Babylon's king, Daniel and his friends could not have been already serving in Nebuchadnezzar's court. They would have been contentedly living their young lives in an independent Judah during Nebuchadnezzar's second year of reign as the king of Babylon.

If the Bible is claiming this dream took place in Nebuchadnezzar's second year of ruling as Babylon's king then the Bible is in clear conflict with itself!

Is this a mistake in the scriptural narrative? Does the Bible carelessly contradict itself in this seemingly simple and straightforward issue? Do we all need to stay up nights worrying about biblical accuracy and credibility? No; not at all.

In stating the fact that it was Nebuchadnezzar's second year of reign the Bible is telling us that it was his second year of reign AFTER the Babylonian destruction of the Holy Temple and the overthrow of Judah.

In other words, the Bible is saying that it was Nebuchadnezzar's second year reigning as the supreme monarch upon the earth, of him reigning as a true, *"king of kings",* as the Bible states of him. *(Daniel 2:37; Ezekiel 26:7)*

The title of, *"king of kings",* is more than fitting for the conqueror of Israel. That is, for the conqueror of the remaining southern Israelite kingdom of Judah and its Davidic monarch who abandoned the majestic right of royal rule in national sin, allowing Babylon and its ruler to come into the fore of world events.

God considers the Babylonian overthrow of Judah and the subsequent destruction of the Holy Temple to be such a pivotal, world altering, event that the Bible (God) chooses to measure the great gentile king Nebuchadnezzar's reign not from the moment he took office as a king in Babylon, but from the point in time He conquered and exiled Judah! For, the defeat of Judah and the destruction of the Holy Temple in Jerusalem was the point at which the, "time(s) of the gentiles", began upon the earth!

The following verses will show us that Nebuchadnezzar's reign as a "normal" monarch was well established years before this statued dream took place in what the Bible refers to as his second year of reign. It was indeed his second year of rule, but it was his second year as the head of the terrible image of empires, an image that had moved into the place of authority in the world of man which had been vacated by the once and yet to be righteous nation of Israel. *(2 Kings chapter 24; 2 Kings 25:8)*

CHAPTER FIVE

WHAT CAN A STATUE DO?

This, *"terrible"*, statue which was shown unto Nebuchadnezzar was that of a man, but it was not just of any man.

It was a combined picture of the great heathen empires of man which were to rule over Adam's children and over the nation of Israel in the time of her exile. But, it was more than just that; it was a picture of all of the combined actions committed by a sinful and fallen mankind throughout the ages. But, it was even more than just that; it was a counterfeit man. It looked like a man, stood like a man, and attempted to rule over man; but it was no man.

Like everything originating outside of the will of God this image had the appearance of something God-made and Godly, but it wasn't real, it had no life in it. It was a false picture of a man.

In all aspects of thought this statue and everything about it was dead. It wasn't the authentic article. This statue could never actually be what it was fabricated to be, for it was made to replicate and imitate something God had created; and no one can ever duplicate the works of God.

This imitation of God's creation was set to assume the position of power originally lost by the first man, Adam. This is a position of power intended by God to be restored unto the last Adam (Messiah) through the nation of promise, Israel; which, like Adam, had also lost its right to rule during this "time of the gentiles" due to its national sin.

This wicked beast of an image was set to inherit man's place of dominion upon the earth due to mankind's errant actions even though God certainly never intended that the image stand as the rightful and supreme authority upon the earth. The statue was a usurper, but not a rightful heir; it was a bullyish pretender to the throne of Adam's lost power. It is that same power which was returned in promise through covenant to the nation of Israel and again lost by Israel for a time.

Now, what can this heathen image which was first revealed unto us in its fullness through a dream given during the second year of Nebuchadnezzar's world encompassing reign tell us?

In order to understand its whole effect, it must first be divided into its individual parts and then each part must be viewed in a spiritual context. For this night vision was a very spiritual dream which spoke about some of the most important issues concerning the era of man upon the earth.

Each individual section of this statue is attempting to control and contort a specific area of mankind's collective life, as well as to dominate and pervert particular areas within an individual person's life. The thoughts, reasoning, emotions, religious and educational activities and outlooks, as well as all other social and financial activities common to man and evident in an individual person's life, from cradle to grave, are constantly being affected, assaulted, assailed, attacked, warped, and manipulated by these high ranking perversional principalities which together form the terrible night image spoken of in the second chapter of Daniel.

These wicked principalities are not mere transient demons which attempt to oppress and possess individuals; they are not even "local" principalities, powers, or rulers which attempt to affect the occupants of their respective cities, towns, regions, and nations. No. These angelic princes of the nations found in the statue of rule are great angelic principal spirits uniquely allowed by God to receive the right of "empire".

Each has a vast array of underlings which work in a tireless quest to blanket God and righteousness from all of mankind and to cover the entire earth in its own specific type of wicked darkness. Their one unifying goal which joins them together in the statue of empire is their

What Can a Statue Do?

desire to rule the lives of Adam's children through an intricate array of deception and illusion which we have been taught to call "normal everyday life".

However, this artificial construct called "normal everyday life" which these principal spirits espouse is a false existence foisted upon the fallen children of man by these purveyors of perversity, and used by them to endlessly manipulate mankind into a vile bondage. The "normal life" known by mankind is a life ruled and orchestrated by these wicked princes of empire which fill Adam's children with desires for the wrong things, priorities, and procedures; it is one which leads all men to exist in a deathish culture of myriad paths, all leading to certain destruction.

THE EPITOME OF THE ADAMIC CURSE IN ACTION

In fact, this wicked statue of satanic sorcery, when viewed in its fullness, represents the epitome of the Adamic curse in action. It is a representative of all those adversarial things which guide mankind into darkness assembled into one place; it is a compilation of such things that were never intended to dominate man. However, the actions of Adam brought these satanic ailments upon the collective body of humanity.

Yes, the statue, and every empire's prince in it, has stood, in a spiritual sense, from the time of Adam's fall readily blanketing the earth with their evil. And, they still stand today through the manifestation of these spiritual principalities involved with each specific nation, and each prince in the statue was, is, and remains a worldwide power in his own area of specialty. But, more so now that Israel has lost its way.

The geographical areas of the empires in question may be ruled by other nations or countries today, and the political entities may be long gone (much as Israel was for well over two thousand years before its amazing return), but the spiritual entities themselves remain. And, they do so with a sobering authority, just as they originally pre-existed the nations and the mankind they so tirelessly seek to rule.

Furthermore, another interesting thing the multihued statue teaches us is that each part of the image, though separate from the others and unique in function, still works together with the others in unity of cause.

The Empires of Image

This is evident in the fact that the empires are depicted together as the many parts of a whole statue and not as separate individual smaller images. This, even though the empires have gone to war against each other in times past as they have competed for individual power and prestige, and the loser begrudgingly had to pass the scepter of strength unto the next chronologically "up and coming" empire within the image .

Each principality in the statue still works together with the others to achieve the overall goal desired by the cabal of satanic conspirators, and that goal is the attainment of complete control over God's creation through their domineering oppression of a mankind once created, *"to tend and keep it". (Genesis 2:15)*

Let's see what the individual sections of this statue can teach us about themselves. Remember now, these great angelic principalities are by no means demons which seek to oppress, possess, and harm individual people. They are the actual "forces" which make the lives and lifestyles of fallen man seem normal and logical to all people.

These wicked princes are those which cause mankind to live the way it has on this earth, rather than living the life God intended for mankind to have: a life He restored unto mankind in His Word, given again to those who repent and believe in His Son, the King Messiah of Israel, the promised seed of the woman who is soon returning in power. *(Hebrews 10:37)*

CHAPTER SIX

BABYLON, ALWAYS WITH THE BABEL

In keeping with the scriptural model, the first part of the statue to be discussed will be the golden head of Babylon.

This empire was not shown as the head of the image for the simple reason that the kingdom of Babylon was chronologically the first of the gentile nations given the right to rule; nor was it the head for the simple reason that it was the greatest and most magnificent kingdom in terms of absolute rule found among the heathen nations of the earth. Both are indeed valid reasons, but there is more to it than that.

There are also spiritual reasons behind Babylon holding that gilded title. The empire of Babylon is the golden head of this manlike statue due to the fact that its angelic principality, the prince spirit of Babylon, is responsible for wickedly and tirelessly affecting (quite proficiently, in point of fact) the unrepentant of mankind in the things of the mind (which is centered in the head).

The soul is his area of expertise, and that angelic spirit is constantly trying to sway all of mankind into deception with his misleading actions which are aimed at the thought life of man. Every child of Adam ever born is affected by the workings of the angel prince of Babylon as he devises countless ways to cloud the mind and darken the soul.

The Empires of Image

Both the believer and unbeliever alike are equally assailed by this principality's deceptive illusions and constant lies, and the saved must be ever watchful that they do not fall into the well hidden pitfalls prepared for them by this wicked Babylonian. His falsities are those which have come to seem so right and normal unto man, but they lead one far from the truth and mercy of God.

"THE BABBLE ON BABYLON"

We can learn some very interesting things about this perverted prince just by looking at the name of the place his principality oversees: Babylon, which is actually called "Babel" in the two Semitic languages of the Bible which are Hebrew and Aramaic.

Aramaic is actually the language much of the Book of Daniel is said to have been originally written in. Aramaic was also the language of use within the kingdom of Babylon as well. And, curiously, like so many of our English words in use today, the English name "Babylon" simply comes to us through the adoption of the Greek rendering of the word. So, English speakers now call this empire "Babylon", according to its Greek pronunciation, rather than using its original Semitic name "Babel".

Interestingly, the name Babel carries two different but conjoined meanings in the two different but conjoined Semitic languages of Hebrew and Aramaic. The name "Babel" hails from the Hebrew word "balal" which means "confusion". This is quite fitting since Babel was the location for the original place of confusion where the confounding of the speech and language of man originally occurred as found in the account of Genesis chapter 11.

The base word of "balal" (confusion) is also quite fitting when looking at the characteristics of this Babylonian angel since the prince spirit of this empire is extremely adept at spreading all manner of confusion and mental disarray into the lives of man.

Contrastingly, in the related, but gentile, language of Aramaic the name "Babel" means "the gate of god"; not necessarily God with a capital "G", but god with a small "g". The small "g" god can refer to any number of things which are incorrectly, and sometimes unknowingly, worshipped as deities such as people, animals, things, concepts, and yes, even errant angels, as is all too often the case.

These two seemingly disparate roots of the word "Babel" which are "confusion" in Hebrew, and "the gate of god" in Aramaic are actually inherently related to each other and interconnected when seen within the context of our spiritual study of this gilded angel prince and his arrogant actions, as we shall soon discover.

However, in order to fully make that discovery we first need to look at the part of man which is specifically impacted and assaulted by the Babylonian principality, and as mentioned, that part is the soul. The soul is the decision-making element of a person. It is the source and location of the thoughts, will, intellect, reason, and emotions of man. It is where both the personality and logical functions of an individual are centered. The soul can be called the real you.

When someone asks: Do you like chocolate or vanilla? Coffee or tea? Warm beaches or snowcapped mountains? Are you an artist, an athlete, an academic, or an individualist? Do you like cars, or horses, or airplanes? It is the soul which makes these decisions and gives people differing unique perspectives and preferences on all issues, many of which we seem to have for no apparent or definable reason other than for choosing them as matters of individual taste.

This Babylonian spirit is the conspirator in charge of blinding the mind and filling it with falsehood, so that individuals would unknowingly make the wrong choices and decisions. Its actions are the chief source of the mental, that is, of the soulish confusion found in the lives of fallen man.

Remember, in the Hebrew language, "Babel" is rooted in the word "balal", which means confusion. The Babylonian spirit effectively causes and then covers mankind in a confused and altered concept of reality, and it does so chiefly by being the heathen Aramaic definition of the word "Babel" which is the "gate of god".

This small "g" god is none other than our angelic acquaintance, the prince of Babylon, the false god which keeps the gate. Using its deceptions it keeps the gate of a person's soul locked and closed unto God and the truth of righteousness and keeps it open to the wicked and perverted lies of satan and his fellow conspirators.

The soul of man, the mind, is the gate to both the body and the spirit of man, and this prince of Babel, acting as the pretentious golden head, clouds the mind with confusion by keeping watch over the gates of the soul. As he does, the body is left open for destruction and the spirit remains imprisoned behind his wretched golden bars.

"IT'S ALL IN THE MIND"

How does the Babylonian accomplish this gilded beguilement?

The answer comes when we receive the answer to our next question:

What are the gates of the soul?

Well, just look at what body parts are found on, and in, the head of a person; the Babylonian does represent and rule over the golden head of the image, after all.

The body parts found on and in the head are: the eyes, the ears, the nose, and the mouth. These are the gates which encompass the final gate of the spirit itself, the very center of the golden head, the brain or mind, which is the physical and tangible component of the soul.

Each of these organs are ways to receive information from the world around us, information which can then be absorbed and processed by the mind, the physical representation of the soul. These organs are our gates through which we receive knowledge of the natural world in which we live. Each gate is guarded and kept by the wicked prince of the gate so that truth would not be known in human life if at all possible.

The prince of Babel keeps the gates of man covered and closed unto the real truth of God and of living God's way. And, he keeps them open to the deceitful golden lies of satan which are constantly and demonically fed to us through these gates of the mind.

Babel's expertise is in the control of the input received, and in the manipulation of the mechanism used for analyzing the data as well. The soul, the mind of man, as part of a being fallen from righteousness in the garden of Eden is kept corrupted by the incessant perversions and twisting of reality fed to it by the evil angel known as the prince of Babylon.

Every "logical" thought of mankind in its fallen state upon this earth has become distorted and corrupted from the intentions of God due to the demonic falsehoods entering the opened gates of man, gates guarded by the Babylonian who instills confusion into the collective existence of mankind.

THE BABYLONIAN TONGUE TWISTER

There is yet one more incredibly important organ found in the head and thusly affected by this particular dark prince. It is the tongue. The tongue releases thought into the physical world; it is the outlet of the soul just as the eyes, ears, mouth, and nose are inlets thereof.

Once the soul (the mind) has absorbed the input it has received through its inlets it will then process that information and use it to make decisions. The soul will also turn that analyzed and processed subject matter back into a physical form, most commonly with the use of the tongue. The old line we've all heard so many times harkens true in this case as well: "What you put into something must come out".

The dominant way for everything to come out of the soul is through the tongue. Speaking unleashes the absorbed and processed data, whether it is good or evil, into the world from whence it came. The prince of Babylon is trying to make sure that the words we unleash into the world are filled with many shrouded evils.

The evil conspirators seek perverted, unsuitable, corrupted ideas and concepts to come flowing from the mouths' of man, words which are ideal for a further spreading of the satanic cloak of deception and darkness placed ever more effectively upon the lives of others. In that way, evil can increase the strength of the satanic bondage already upon people.

In releasing corrupt speech into the world those of fallen mankind who do so have become the unwitting servants of this angelic principality, further intensifying the thickness of his blanket of illusion under which others sadly live.

Speaking about this subject the Bible says it the following way:

> *"O generation of vipers, how can ye, being evil, speak good things? For out of the abundance of the heart the mouth speaketh." (Matthew 12:34)*

The heart spoken of in this previous verse is one affected by the evils buffeting the soul, the mind; it is the very central part of man which houses the thoughts that are subsequently spoken and released into God's creation.

The prophetic account of the statue does not indicate where the divisional line between the metals of gold and silver occurred in the image, but logic would lend itself toward the notion that the neck is considered to be more a part of the golden head than it is of the silver arms and breast.

In that vein (or should we say artery?), a neck of gold would also be most in keeping with the identified operational jurisdiction of this Babylonian spirit. For the neck is instrumental as a part of a determining mechanism, and as we have seen, the soul is *the* quintessential determining mechanism in man.

The neck turns the head, allowing the body to go a certain direction. Its movement also lets the eyes see things around the person, the ears to hear sound from different directions, the nose to sniff around more effectively (admittedly, quite droll), and the mouth to speak into the determined area of one's choosing. The neck also contains the throat which enables the tongue to transmit words; the throat also passes what the mouth has consumed down into the body for digestion.

All of these functions of the neck are important for the prince of Babylon to have as he tirelessly attempts to lead mankind astray, guiding the children of men into a world dominated by perverted thoughts which seem right in our eyes; but they actually dim our knowledge of truth and restrict our ability to bring forth the will of God.

In that the Aramaic meaning of Babel is "the gate of god" we can see that this angelic gatekeeper has behaved in precisely that way. He has watched the gate of the soul to shut God out of the minds' of men so that people can focus on the seemingly "more important things" which the satanic conspirators would incessantly feed us as they seek to fill our souls with treachery and confusion.

The confusing Babylonian prince, the one who controls the "gate of god", would have us worship any and all other "gods" except the real One.

One of the most effective soul covering blankets used by this Babylonian is the notion of effort for the exclusive benefit of self, which since the fall of man has been engraved into each person and actually pressed into the entire construct of the physical creation.

Everything about self effort seems so logical to us, but it leads nowhere. Self effort is the product of the incorrect (confused) realization that we can manipulate ourselves and the world around us to bring otherwise unattainable benefits unto us. It roots itself in taking instead of giving, vanity rather than humility, and lust instead of love.

This Babylonian has mankind doing mental gymnastics of all sorts in order to have man place a faux justification on human pride. It tells us that we can trust in our senses and fill our minds with only the input coming from the natural world, a tainted world we are unnaturally led to believe we are subject to.

Babylon teaches us to disregard the True God and the grace He provides. All the while the dark angel is attempting to sway us into a captivity based on a wisdom not of God. It is a wisdom of the senses; this deviancy is akin to the one which originally caused the wicked angels to transgress so long ago, and is the same which swayed Eve into darkness back, *"in the beginning"*. It says: I need, I want, I can, I must, I will; and its thoughts leave God and His will out of our lives as we attempt to make ourselves better and more successful at the expense of His ways.

As we have seen, the principality of Babylon is specifically in charge of interfering with the things of the mind of man; that is to say, it operates in the perverse cloaking actions of the satanic conspiracy as they affect the human soul.

The thoughts and actions which are so natural to us, yet constantly lead to hurt and defeat, are the product of this angelic prince and his various vassals confusing the mind and darkening the soul. This they accomplish with the efficiency of a well conducted orchestra, and mankind exists in the foggy daze of distorted thinking totally unaware of the confusing and perverted actions taken by the prince of Babylon to bring harm unto man and separate God's created from His love.

Every thought of man is either rooted in a holy God, or in a wicked and satanically induced sin. There is literally no other place of conception for thoughts; there is no independent neutral element in existence for man to draw knowledge from other than these two sources. And, it is this golden-headed element of Babylon which seeks to, and does, blind the soul of man in confusion, causing man to prefer wickedness and death over holiness and life. Since the fall of Adam its thoughts have become ours, its deceptions our reality.

If you have a question, the prince of Babylon is ready with an answer. For he rules the gates of the soul manipulating the everyday life of fallen Adam's children with a wickedness beyond their own knowledge, adding yoke to yoke, burden to burden, and promise to promise; until all which brings death seems right in the minds of man.

Babylon offers the desire for self effort, it cries: "You can do it." "You can find what you need in the natural world just look for it.", whispers the well skilled angel in your ear.

Religion? Sure, Babylon has got you covered there as well. In fact, the Bible in stating that the head of the statue was of gold was making exactly this point, for gold scripturally represents religious and "spiritual" matters, which are issues that are judged by, and most deeply affect, the soul.

The golden prince is the foremost purveyor of religions, creeds, and dogmas of every variety. Just take your pick; the world is full of an infinite array of "manmade" religions which offer you as much work as you can handle.

The effort you put out to religiously "better" yourself will allow you to feel justified in your own eyes, and the knowledge you acquire will give you great pride in yourself, but it is all deception. It's a golden deception contrived by a wicked brilliance to weaken Adam's children lest they return unto the Lord their God and be healed, freed from the yoke of this enemy of the soul and his likeminded comrades.

Remember, gold in scripture is representative of religious, that is, of spiritual matters. It stands for the things of the highest value, the sacred; this Babylonian with his place as the golden head of a false man is well situated to promote and establish the false illusion of "golden" religions among those of Adam clenched within his grasp.

Psalm 143 is devoted to the subject of the afflicted soul being persecuted by a tireless enemy. As the soul seeks the mercies of God he cries out to learn God's ways, ways which have been hidden from him through the darkness of the wicked ones. One verse from Psalm 143 follows, but an in-depth study of the entire chapter is recommended:

> *"For the enemy hath persecuted my soul; he hath smitten my life down to the ground; he hath made me to dwell in darkness, as those that have been long dead." (Psalm 143:3)*

DON'T THINK LIKE A BABYLONIAN!

The good news is we CAN return to God. As individuals we can repent of the lies we have believed and lived for so long; we can stop living in a house of corrupt cards and vapid veils. The battle for the mind is won at the cross of Calvary, and the soul can find the answers to the truths it needs in Yeshua (Jesus), the King Messiah, the One who has given us a sound mind and rest for the soul. *(2 Timothy 1:7)*

The Babylonian prince's power is no longer legitimately in place over those who are redeemed by the King of the Jews. Those who are saved have become new creations in Messiah Jesus, and there is no principality which can override the authority of the earth's rightful King. The lies of Babel cannot keep bound those made free in Messiah.

> *"Therefore if any man [be] in Christ, [he is] a new creature: old things are passed away; behold, all things are become new." (2 Corinthians 5:17)*

The confusion causing guardian of the gate, the prince of the portals, must bow before the conquering King. Yes, we must constantly be vigilant and grow into the knowledge of God through His Spirit and His Word, but He will help us there as well, as we await the day Babylon is finally judged and destroyed.

The following verse gives us some insight into Babylon's last moments:

> "And a mighty angel took up a stone like a great millstone, and cast [it] into the sea, saying, Thus with violence shall that great city Babylon be thrown down, and shall be found no more at all." (Revelation 18:21)

The following verse will show us the importance of being transformed through the renewing of the mind as we place ourselves under the authority of Israel's King and become free from the golden yokes of satan's design. Actually, all of Romans chapter 12 speaks about how not to be influenced by wickedness and its lies. Certainly this gilded Babylonian prince is foremost among the purveyors of such iniquity:

> "I beseech you therefore, brethren, by the mercies of God, that ye present your bodies a living sacrifice, holy, acceptable unto God, [which is] your reasonable service. And be not conformed to this world: but be ye transformed by the renewing of your mind, that ye may prove what [is] that good, and acceptable, and perfect, will of God." (Romans 12:1-2)

"MIND" YOUR MANNERS

AKA

"DON'T EAT THIS BABYLONIAN SOUL FOOD!"

Yet another way to learn more about the operational conduct and traits of this angelic prince of empire is to look at the culture and characteristics of the nation he originally presided over as the ruling principality, the nation which carried more of his attributes than any other, and that, of course, is the nation of Babylon itself.

What are the defining characteristics of Babylon?

The single greatest world altering event which occurred in Babylon (pre-Nebuchadnezzar) was the confusion of languages. The weakened and altered thought processes and communicational abilities of the mind (the soul) came about as a result of the actions that occurred in the land which was under the political reign of the Babylonian.

That action occurred as this spirit tried to overreach his authority and unduly influence mankind in order to permanently darken man's existence through the full Adamic implementation of the one thing he had the most intimate knowledge of, and that one thing is control.

It was during the time in which the earth's population existed under the political rule of the nation presided over by this Babylonian prince (*Genesis chapter 11*) that the strongest attempt was made to control Adam's children through a "manmade" religious and political system.

The Babylonian control of the political and religious systems of the world is the greatest and most enduring burden which this angel prince has been able to place upon fallen mankind.

The stamp of the Babylonian remains strongly pressed into the customs and cultures of every major religious and political system in the world to this day, affecting everything from cultures to calendars, and all things in between. Every religious and political system ever adopted by man has elements of the original perversions of the soul first implemented by man in Babylon.

Those who come into contact with "religious" knowledge will unavoidably cross paths with the effects and actions of this soul perverting spirit; its tenets are universal, and its rules are always the same, regardless of religion or philosophy.

A few examples of these gilded Babylonian cages are found in the following phrases: "Sacrifice", "Make yourself better", "Be a good person", "Suffer for your 'god'", "Look down on the less initiated (but never admit to doing so)", and, "Always, always, always, have someone you can revere standing between you and your deity".

This Babylon is more than just an historical footnote. It's more than just a power hungry nation. It's more than just a political or religious source of perversions. Babylon is a spiritual world power which heads up (quite literally, pardon the pun) a unique conspiracy of angelic evil epitomized by the statue of Nebuchadnezzar's dream.

This conspiracy is one which has seized control of all aspects of "normal human life" common to natural fallen mankind. And, for the most part, we as people are blinded to the depth of his confusing control.

In fact, the perversional characteristics of the false existence of life developed by the wicked angelic conspirators and then foisted upon fallen mankind by the angelic princes of empire, Babylon foremost among them, cause mankind to become unable to understand the first thing about the true life God intended for man to have.

BABYLON; IT GIVES ALL "HARLOTS" A BAD NAME

AKA

"WHEN IS A WHORE NOT SO GREAT?"

Speaking of Babylon, the prophet Isaiah decrees the following:

> *"...for thou shalt no more be called, The lady of kingdoms."* (Isaiah 47:5)

The characteristics of this "golden" spirit, the one who is the confusion causing keeper of the gate, and its insidious effects upon mankind are precisely what have earned Babylon the biblical title of the "great whore".

Yes, it's true that the Bible has referred to other nations, empires, spirits, people, entities, and their deceptive constructs as "whores", or has said that they practice "whoredoms", or said that they have gone "a whoring" etc., but no other entity of any kind is called the "great whore". That is a title reserved only, and specifically, for Babylon.

This spiritual pervert is not content in dooming its own self by its actions. No. Babylon is fixated on enticing as many of the children of Adam into destruction as possible through the use of its alluring false charms and perverted promises which are found in the artificial world created by the satanic conspirators.

Babylon, the system of rule as instituted by that spirit, is unquestionably the biggest whore of them all, and the angel prince of Babylon can best be described as the biggest pimp.

A LOVELESS LIE

In order to receive more insight into this unseemly Babylonian entity we need to ask the following biblically based question:

What exactly is a whore?

It is essentially a person who pretends to be something she is not in order to entice others into a perversional and detrimental activity to gain possessions from them. The whore is a fallacy; it is an illusionary loveless lie, a false image of something other than what it is.

It is, in fact, an extremely twisted perversion of a wife. It may be externally constituted the same way; it may even look essentially the same or even better than what a wife would appear to outwardly be. It may claim to offer the false promises of otherwise unattainable joy and pleasure, but it sells a temporal deception offering a version of life which can never come to pass in reality. And, it never seeks to bring about life; in fact, its implicit goal is not to.

This specific whore known as Babylon has successfully enchanted the whole of Adam's fallen family with its captivating calls and siren songs that offer glamorous and glittering goblets of gaiety and marvelous moments of myrrh, but its deceptive ways lead to poverty, destruction, and death on all levels of existence in existence. The lies of Babylon help constitute the deceptive world in which mankind lives today.

The betraying beauty of religious endeavors, the coaxing call of self effort, the seductive sound of the seemingly logical things portrayed as God and its self derived holiness; Babylon has brought unto man a painted picture of potential pleasure which constantly bombards the mind (the soul) with a false promise of pleasure that will never come to pass. For, its one-dimensional ways are nothing more than an intricate array of illusions which lead to increased bondage and certain death.

Remember, the whore is a lie offering for a price something it truly cannot give, and it always, always, always pretends to be something it is not.

What is the price this greatest of harlots charges for the illusion of her charms?

Only the highest price a person can pay: Babylon demands your very soul.

Sadly, it is in the arms of this demonic deception of satanic sacrilege that a fallen mankind has found itself most comfortable, blinded, broken, and betrayed as was the Nazarite Samson in his darkest day; but unlike him, void of even the knowledge of its own corrupt condition, communally lacking the wisdom to cry out in repentance unto the God of all creation and to accept His gift of freedom and life. Should the collective be unwilling, let us then turn, one by one, and bow ourselves unto the King Messiah.

Speaking of Babylon, the whore, the Bible says the following:

> "Babylon [hath been] a golden cup in the LORD'S hand, that made all the earth drunken: the nations have drunken of her wine; therefore the nations are mad."(Jeremiah 51:7)

> "And there followed another angel, saying, Babylon is fallen, is fallen, that great city, because she made all nations drink of the wine of the wrath of her fornication." (Revelation 14:8)

> "And there came one of the seven angels which had the seven vials, and talked with me, saying unto me, Come hither; I will shew unto thee the judgment of the great whore that sitteth upon many waters: With whom the kings of the earth have committed fornication, and the inhabitants of the earth have been made drunk with the wine of her fornication. So he carried me away in the spirit into the wilderness: and I saw a woman sit upon a scarlet coloured beast, full of names of blasphemy, having seven heads and ten horns. And the woman was arrayed in purple and scarlet colour, and decked with gold and precious stones and pearls, having a golden cup in her hand full of abominations and filthiness of her fornication: And upon her forehead [was] a name written, MYSTERY, BABYLON THE GREAT, THE MOTHER OF HARLOTS AND ABOMINATIONS OF THE EARTH." (Revelation 17:1-5)

"THE LAND OF THE NORTH"

Zechariah, the honored prophet of God, explicitly makes the following enlightening statement concerning Babylon:

> "Ho, ho, [come forth], and flee from the land of the north, saith the LORD: for I have spread you abroad as the four winds of

the heaven, saith the LORD. Deliver thyself, O Zion, that dwellest [with] the daughter of Babylon." (Zechariah 2:6-7)

This, *"land of the north"*, which spins the people of the earth into a satanically designed web of captivity is none other than the infamous, *"daughter of Babylon"*, spoken of in the pages of scripture.

While not every reference to a "north" land or country is directed specifically toward Babylon it is nevertheless the unique and specific, *"land of the north"*. It is the very same which has been the place of spiritual imprisonment and captivity for the children of Adam; and prophetically speaking, it has been the specific place of exile and banishment for the nation of Israel as a whole.

Remember, Babylon is more than just a geographical place or a political entity; it is a spiritual construct, and it is the very workings of the angel prince of Babylon himself. For he is the "confusion" causing keeper of "the gate of god". And, when the Bible speaks of Israel's eventual return from, *"the land of the north"*, it is specifically referring to the coming judgment and destruction of Babylon taking place, and of Israel's need to distance herself from Babylon in all possible ways.

In that coming judgment we will find the end of the Hebrew exile and Israel's full return unto the will of God, unto the land of Promise, and unto the role which that nation was always meant to have. As a result of this, all of the captives of Adam found in Babylon shall be set free of her bonds. *(Jeremiah 50:18-20)*

> *"O daughter of Babylon, who art to be destroyed; happy [shall he be], that rewardeth thee as thou hast served us. Happy [shall he be], that taketh and dasheth thy little ones against the stones." (Psalm 137:8-9)*

EVERYONE SHOULD BE SO HAPPY!

To that, we can only say, AMEN!

CHAPTER SEVEN

PERSIA, MORE THAN JUST GREAT CARPETS

The second empire to be looked at is naturally the second one mentioned in the scriptural sequence given in the terrible statue and that, of course, is the arms and breast of silver: Media-Persia.

This well armed Persian prince is certainly no push-over (pardon the pun). Persia's place in the statue confirms that, as does the valuable metal of silver of which these physically important empire body parts are composed.

This place of high standing within the statue of man that is held by the silver Persian prince is well indicative of its rule over the very precious spirit of fallen man. The enslavement of the subjugated spirit of man is his fiendish forte. And, not to be outdone by any other perverted principality of pretentiousness, this sterling satrap is well versed in schemes which are intended to cost mankind plenty; for his heady works are designed to smother the life, the spirit, of Adam's race.

Interestingly, in the language of the Bible, Hebrew, and indeed, in a great many of the languages and cultures found in the world, including Aramaic, silver is synonymous with money; the word is the same and its usage in dialogue is fully interchangeable. The Hebrew word for both "money" and "silver" is "kesef".

What exactly does that tell us about the Persian's role in things?

Well, silver, that is, money, is the proof and measure of one's wealth. It is the evidence of an individual's financial strength and abilities, and is, in this Persian case, the perverted natural counterpart of the strength of the spirit of man. For the spirit of a being is the life, ability, power, capability, and empowerment of a being; the inherent rights of an individual to be and to do, the mobilizing force.

The existence of the spirit can be classified as the confirmed evidence of an individual's life witnessed in the works done. Whereas silver (money) is the confirmation of an individual's ability to purchase, own, and affect things; it is the evidence of an individual's ability and work. In this spiritual sense, silver is a picture of the fallen spirit of mankind and of the corrupt power which resides as a principality over it.

This high-ranking angel prince of Persia ceaselessly works on the spirit of man to make man stand at enmity with God. Resistance is his specialty, strength his renown. This fact is borne out and explained by the unique location he holds within the statue. The Persian prince rules over the double kingdom of Media-Persia, and he is thusly well envisioned as controlling the two arms of the statue, the right and the left, the stronger and the one less so.

These arms, like all arms, can and are used to resist: to fight with, to wrestle against, and to resist. The Persian prince fights from the heart and for the heart; he wrestles against any and all who come to uphold and advance the truth of God and His will. The specific mission of this silver armed angel is to hold God's will and His coming Messiah at bay. This silver prince is the arms of the satanic conspiracy in the world of man, arms are used for wrestling and for combat; without arms the soldier is helpless. However, the conspiracy of the wicked is well armed with this Persian in their ranks.

So vital is this Persian to the satanic war machine that without him in the transgressionary battle against Godliness and man upon the earth the satanic conspirators would be near defenseless and powerless in the battle for man's authority. Babylon's actions aided in the dethronement of Israel, but Persia will do all in its power to keep Israel down and out.

The Persian prince does all in his power to resist the inevitable Kingdom of Messiah from appearing upon the earth. Whether in the heart and life of an individual or in fullness across the entire breadth of the earth through the restoration of the physical kingdom of Israel; it matters naught to him. He will eagerly resist all Godliness wherever it is found.

In so doing, he will provide a false alternate form of existence, one which ties the individual in an ever more insidious knot. Being the two arms of the silvery image this principality will provide mankind with the illusional ability to work for one's own righteousness.

Working for one's own betterment and holiness has been the goal of man ever since Eve first bit into the fruit of the tree of the knowledge of good and evil in her misguided attempt to attain the unattainable. This Persian prince is well armed with his silvery evidence of ability and work, but the wealth of a works based righteousness will always prove more slippery than silver in a drunkard's hand.

THE SONNET OF SILVER

AKA

"A SILVER LIE-NING"

In seeing that the breast of the statue was silver, along with the arms, it means that the organs which the breast of man contains are also under the influence of this dark angel prince. Naturally, the first organ of the breast that will be mentioned is the heart.

The heart is the source and center of human life. It is also scripturally the foundation and core of spiritual life and it is the one thing which must first be given over to and yielded unto God before any other. Without the heart (spirit) placed in right standing with God there can be no life.

This Persian is set to make sure that such a thing as the humbling of the heart unto God and the rebirth of the spirit of man does not happen. He seeks to, and has, hardened the hearts of mankind against the Lord and against all things Godly as he gives the fallen children of Adam a seemingly natural deadness and resistance to the rightful rule of God over themselves.

satan knows that the currency (remember, in Hebrew silver means money or currency) of a dead heart (spirit) is worth much to the wicked conspirators, and this well armed prince is just the one to keep man's spirit dead by holding God, Messiah, and His Kingdom at arm's length and away from Adam's children.

As gold was to the head, silver is to the heart. Gold is the deceptive and confusing self-effort of rebellion which mankind holds in all ways, especially religious; and silver is biblically most indicative of money, which is wealth, power, and ability. The silver Persian prince has effectively filled the hearts of mankind with an incredible yearning for personal wealth and power, and deadened Adam's children unto God, the All Sufficient One.

In doing so, the Persian gives mankind an illusion of ability, added to the thought that work (both spiritual and physical) can attain the Babylonian golden utopia for oneself. This errant angel of empire knows a heart so corrupted has no place for a just God, and it will have no desire to humble itself unto Him. Such a heart believes that it has all the answers in the pride of life and in the deceitfulness of riches, both physical and spiritual, and it will resist God to its very end. *(1 John 2:16)*

The heart is the source of love, but with a dead spirit, one subjugated to a hardness instituted by the Persian, the heart cannot love; for such a heart is not truly alive. The Persian knows that his most effective form of resistance, and remember, this angel is most renowned for his effective arms of resistance, is to keep the hearts of mankind dead and thusly distant from the life and love of God. And so, all who are left with these loveless silvery hearts add to, and expand, the rule of spiritual darkness over a bitterly burdened and enslaved humanity.

There is yet one more set of vital organs which belong to the silvery breast, and that is the lungs. The lungs supply the entire body with the essential oxygen it needs, and in doing so, the lungs provide the body with the power necessary to function and exist. Existence is exactly what the Persian controls as the presumptive overlord of the spirit.

How fitting for the lungs to be in the statue's breast of silver under the control of the Medo-Persian prince's dual kingdom, for there are also two lungs in the body! They are a duo, just as the Medo-Persian double empire is; and almost too amazingly, just as the double empire has one partner smaller in size than the other, anatomical study teaches us that the left lung of a person is also smaller than the right! WOW! God sure knows how to make a great point!

Interestingly, the lungs are also an important co-operative element binding these great empires of image together, for they work in tandem with the mouth of the golden head giving it the ability to bring forth words and to express thought. To say that the wicked conspirators work together is really an understatement, and this statue proves that point. They not only work together they are in sworn covenant with one another, and their great scheme is dependent on their close cooperation with each other.

Everything about this Persian prince speaks of power and strength, and most of all, ability; including its unique position in the statue. It is the arms of resistance, the heart which is the center of (perverted) life, and the lungs which strengthen the body (of satanic opposition) and help give voice to evil. Lastly, it is silver, money, the measure of work and the evidence of effort. The Persian is the prince of illusional ability and pride which binds the spirit into serving the will of the satanic conspiracy.

THE PERSIAN POWERPLAY

The Bible, in fact, gives us a very telling depiction of the Prince of Persia, illuminating unto us the audacity, gall, and power which this angel has to resist even the direct messenger of the Most High God.

Yes, the Bible shows this Persian prince boldly and defiantly resisting the mighty one of the Lord, and doing so with a surprising amount of success for a time. The full account of this remarkable event is found in the tenth chapter of the Book of Daniel. The entire chapter will be looked at next.

Don't worry, it isn't a long chapter!

Daniel chapter ten:

> *10:1 "In the third year of Cyrus king of Persia a thing was revealed unto Daniel, whose name was called Belteshazzar; and the thing [was] true, but the time appointed [was] long:*

and he understood the thing, and had understanding of the vision."

10:2 "In those days I Daniel was mourning three full weeks."

10:3 "I ate no pleasant bread, neither came flesh nor wine in my mouth, neither did I anoint myself at all, till three whole weeks were fulfilled."

10:4 "And in the four and twentieth day of the first month, as I was by the side of the great river, which [is] Hiddekel;"

10:5 "Then I lifted up mine eyes, and looked, and behold a certain man clothed in linen, whose loins [were] girded with fine gold of Uphaz:"

10:6 "His body also [was] like the beryl, and his face as the appearance of lightning, and his eyes as lamps of fire, and his arms and his feet like in colour to polished brass, and the voice of his words like the voice of a multitude."

10:7 "And I Daniel alone saw the vision: for the men that were with me saw not the vision; but a great quaking fell upon them, so that they fled to hide themselves."

10:8 "Therefore I was left alone, and saw this great vision, and there remained no strength in me: for my comeliness was turned in me into corruption, and I retained no strength."

10:9 "Yet heard I the voice of his words: and when I heard the voice of his words, then was I in a deep sleep on my face, and my face toward the ground.

10:10 "And, behold, an hand touched me, which set me upon my knees and [upon] the palms of my hands."

10:11 "And he said unto me, O Daniel, a man greatly beloved, understand the words that I speak unto thee, and stand upright: for unto thee am I now sent. And when he had spoken this word unto me, I stood trembling."

10:12 "Then said he unto me, Fear not, Daniel: for from the first day that thou didst set thine heart to understand, and to chasten thyself before thy God, thy words were heard, and I am come for thy words."

10:13 "But the prince of the kingdom of Persia withstood me one and twenty days: but, lo, Michael, one of the chief princes, came to help me; and I remained there with the kings of Persia."

10:14 "Now I am come to make thee understand what shall befall thy people in the latter days: for yet the vision [is] for [many] days."

10:15 "And when he had spoken such words unto me, I set my face toward the ground, and I became dumb."

10:16 "And, behold, [one] like the similitude of the sons of men touched my lips: then I opened my mouth, and spake, and said unto him that stood before me, O my lord, by the vision my sorrows are turned upon me, and I have retained no strength."

10:17 "For how can the servant of this my lord talk with this my lord? for as for me, straightway there remained no strength in me, neither is there breath left in me."

10:18 "Then there came again and touched me [one] like the appearance of a man, and he strengthened me,"

10:19 "And said, O man greatly beloved, fear not: peace [be] unto thee, be strong, yea, be strong. And when he had spoken unto me, I was strengthened, and said, Let my lord speak; for thou hast strengthened me."

10:20 "Then said he, Knowest thou wherefore I come unto thee? and now will I return to fight with the prince of Persia: and when I am gone forth, lo, the prince of Grecia shall come."

10:21 "But I will shew thee that which is noted in the scripture of truth: and [there is] none that holdeth with me in these things, but Michael your prince."

In the preceding Bible chapter we once again find Daniel, an exiled and subjugated son of Israel, who by this time had served in both the

Babylonian and Persian kingdoms as a high ranking advisor and counselor to kings. The wisdom of Daniel was held in great esteem by the leadership of both ruling empires, but he was still a Jew and a lover of his people, as such, he sought the Lord his God for the deliverance of Israel, and for knowledge concerning the coming events thereof.

Daniel had embarked upon a time of fasting and prayer unto God in humble supplication for knowledge concerning the redemption of his nation. He knew that the redemption was unquestionably promised, but he was seeking a deeper understanding of God's intended actions so that he and others could better work and pray towards God's intended result.

On the twenty-first day of his fast a being of great glory appeared unto Daniel to bring him the prayed for and requested information. Interestingly, this great being had set out with the answer immediately after Daniel first prayed, but it took this messenger twenty-one days to arrive with the message.

Since God sent forth the answer immediately after Daniel first prayed for it, why did it take so long for Daniel to receive the answer to his prayer?

This is a question of legal rights and authorities. The angel prince of Persia, who held sway over the ruling empire of the day, also had control over the subjugated house of Israel and had particular rights over Persian residents such as Daniel. This prince was adamantly resisting the Godly messenger which he perceived to be wrongfully intruding into his area of control.

There was a legal conflict afoot between these two parties, between the messenger of God and the prince of Persia. The ruling Persian prince with his legitimate claims on the rights to restrict spiritual activities in his territory was vying against the glorious messenger of the Almighty who was operating within his God sanctioned anointings and mandate to deliver God's Word unto His servant Daniel.

First of all, let's see what type of messenger this was. This great and glorious being was not the angel Gabriel, Daniel had seen the angel Gabriel before, and would have recognized him in this instance as well.

Secondly, this wasn't Israel's archangel Michael, for Michael later came to strengthen this great being against Persia's prince.

Thirdly, this was not another angel. Daniel mentions another being who accompanied this great one; the other was, *"...like the similitude of the sons of men..."*, that is, the other being was an angel, but the great one was clearly not, *"...like the similitude of the sons of men...".*

He was something else, greater than man and greater than angels. Was this an "Old Testament" appearance by the Messiah Himself, come to deliver the message of Israel's return personally? I, myself, believe so. However, even this great Godly being was hindered by the conspiratorial, but legally ruling, angel prince of Persia from attending to God's work in the areas of Persian control.

How could this "mere" angel prince resist and delay the righteous messenger of the Most High God from speaking with a greatly beloved servant of the Lord?

Well, the prince of Persia was appointed by God unto his place of power, and barring any illegalities on his behalf he was more than within his rights to be there and to resist unwanted spiritual activity in his area of authority. The Persian had every right to demand that such unwanted intrusions not take place in his area of rule, which was the Persian empire; and Daniel along with all of Israel was under the rule of the Persian empire, placed their at the behest of God Himself.

God cannot contradict Himself in Word or in deed, so this issue of seemingly contradictive angelic authorities, as seen in this standoff, came to a head in front of the Holy Judge (God Himself). It was in the context of that legal setting that Michael, the angel Prince of Israel, was able to bring aid to the great messenger.

Israel, though subject to Persia, was still found to be a nation, and as such it still had certain unique rights inherent to it. One such right was determined by God to be the right to receive information on the duration and manner of its captivity and exile, and the eventual end thereof. In other words, God had to judge favorably on behalf of His messenger in order for Daniel (Israel) to be able to receive this prophetic revelation.

Let's put it this way: legal Persian fire had to be fought with legal Israeli fire. The messenger needed Michael's input and authority in the successful fulfillment of this matter. Michael's anointings as Israel's angel prince had proven invaluable in the settling of the dispute of the legalities involved with the messenger's mission into Persian territory and his right to bring Daniel the message concerning Israel's future.

In keeping with this thought, the great messenger said to Daniel, in the book of Daniel 10:21,: *"...and [there is] none that holdeth with me in these things, but Michael your prince."*. Michael, the angel prince of Israel, was the only angel who came to aid the messenger because he was the only righteous angel who could help in this specific situation. Michael was the only one with the particular anointings (assignments) necessary to assist this great messenger on his quest to deliver unto Daniel the Word of God concerning captive Israel.

It wasn't a question of God's other angels being too lazy or too weak to fight the Persian and to aid the great messenger, but in this particular matter they did not hold the necessary authority to be of benefit to the messenger in the implementation of his mission.

The point to be made in this look at the methodology of the Persian prince is that power, strength, and tenacity are his attributes of character (as epitomized by the two arms, heart, and lungs of the statue); and he does not hesitate to use them freely to resist and block the will of God from taking place in every possible way. Even if it entails resisting the great messenger of God Himself in order to do so.

THE PROSE OF PERSIA

AKA

"HOT UNDER THE (SILVERY) COLLAR"

To receive more information about the way the angelic price of Persia works, and to better understand the particular attributes of darkness which he spreads among man, we need go no further than to the nation which he rules; the one which is thusly most in tune with this angelic prince.

That nation, of course, is Persia itself. Persia is a nation which held strength and order in high regard. In times of war Persia often used force of numbers to overwhelm its enemies; ingenious battle tactics were secondary to sheer strength and disciple in this nation turned empire.

It was also in Persia that the "fire worship" associated with Zoroastrianism first gained wide popularity among people. Fire was seen as the ultimate physical power as it was capable of destroying or altering nearly everything it comes into contact with. Again, power was very highly valued in Persian society.

Most interesting, however, was the way in which the Persians viewed their king. The Persian king was not an all powerful monarch in the traditional sense, as was the Babylonian and many of the other ancient royals of absolute authority. The Persian king was actually himself subject to one other authority; the king was bound to his own spoken word. Once the king had given a decree he could not rescind it or alter it.

The king, the court, and the entire nation were bound by the king's word, whatever it may have been. The word of the Persian king was in that way seen as the highest authority in the land, and even the king himself was subject to it. Briefly put, the Persian culture didn't respect the person of the king as much as they respected his word, his law, and his position. Examples of this can be found scripture. *(Daniel chapter 6; The Book of Ester)*

> *"Now, O king, establish the decree and sign the writing, so that it cannot be changed, according to the law of the Medes and Persians, which does not alter." (Daniel 6:8)*

The supremacy of the Persian king's word over all things, even over the king himself, was remarkably similar to the way the Bible describes God's relationship to His own Word.

God, the Creator of the universe, is biblically shown to be obligated to carry out and respect the Words He has previously uttered. In such a way, His Word is the final and absolute authority over all things as it restricts all beings and obligates even God Himself to carry out His previously stated will. *(Psalm 138:2; Isaiah 46:11; Jeremiah 4:28; Ezekiel 24:14)*

It seems that the Persians chose to learn of, and then implement, some very important spiritual characteristics into their national culture. In this strength loving society the word of the king was seen as the ultimate power.

Yet another unusual parallel can be drawn between the monarch of Persia and a being of uniquely high position, and that, of course, is the

Messiah. This parallel is one which the Bible itself makes. One of the Persian kings, Cyrus, is actually called "messiah" by God through the prophet Isaiah. *(Isaiah 45:1)*

This Persian king is, in fact, the only gentile to be called "messiah" (which means "anointed") in the pages of scripture. That is a title which speaks of great strength and authority granted by God for a set purpose.

Persia, its culture, its king, and his word, stand for strength, strength, strength. This is in true keeping with the Medo-Persian empire's place as the empire nation of the silvery angelic prince; the one who rules the arms, chest, lungs, and heart of the dread night image. He tirelessly adds his power to the rule of wickedness over man.

TAKE HEART!

(Pun intended!)

Do not let this Persian harden your hearts any longer! The Lord God of Israel has promised that if we turn to Him He will take away our hard (perhaps, silvery stone?) hearts and give us hearts of flesh. He will give us hearts that are no longer influenced by this silver spooned deceiver and his satanic comrades.

Let's give God our hearts and our lives, living for Him through the power of His Son, Yeshua (Jesus), the Anointed King! *(Ezekiel 11:19, 36:26)*

CHAPTER EIGHT

GREECE, IT'S CERTAINLY NOT A HEALTH FOOD

The third kingdom to be revealed in the statue is none other than Greece.

This empire is seen as the belly and thighs of brass, the formidable midsection of the terrible standing image. The Grecian prince is the spiritual subjugator whose actions are most familiar to all people, for the bonds of this errant angel are easily fitted to, and borne, on the weary bones and bruised flesh of the oppressed masses of a fallen mankind. That is the reason the empire of this prince is portrayed as the very center of the statue, but man's overt familiarity with this prince and his modes of conduct conceal his strength.

Simply put, the prince of Greece is the keeper of the ways of the flesh; thusly, he has a great proficiency in the seminal deceptions of the physical world. His bonds include all things pertaining to the wants of physical life as known by the children of the fallen Adam. And, "physical life", in essence, is the only type of life a natural unsaved person can ever truly know.

Natural man (actually, natural man is, scripturally speaking, an *unnatural* state of being) knows only of the physical and its needs. From ambition to laziness, lust to love, poverty to wealth, culture to barbarism, anorexia to gluttony, stupidity to intelligence, and ignorance to education; the Grecian angel strings mankind along in a never ending list of fleshly issues and pursuits contrived to both increase and please the yearnings of the body as ruled by the brass belly.

The core location of the Greek empire in Nebuchadnezzar's statue explains the critical role of all physical and self pleasing behaviors in the workings of this "prince of the flesh". His wicked influence is amply seen in mankind as a whole and in the lives of individual people in particular. This "Greecy bellied" location also shows the central importance of all carnality in the satanic scheme of human conquest.

Just how important is this Grecian potentate's empire to the satanic schemes of the wicked angelic conspirators?

They are extremely important! For the area he rules within the statue represents the life of man's flesh, the physical aspects of mankind's existence. When the triune being, Adam (mankind), sinned in the garden of Eden and partook of the forbidden fruit mankind died spiritually in that very same instant. With the spirit of man in a state of death, the only part left to influence the decision making soul was the body, which was given over to eventual death during that same fruit filled Edenic episode.

Consequently, the flesh, and its Edenically received perverted death-loving physical outlook, became central to mankind's sordid state of being. Without this Grecian in charge of his office over the ways of the flesh of man the satanic conspirators couldn't work their schemes of control; for fallen man now lives solely through the carnal.

In other words, the Grecian, with his empire, is the lynchpin upon which the entire cabal of conspirators depends. This is well expressed in his rule over the centrally located belly. The entire cabal of satanic wickedness is dependent upon the Grecian's unique role as the upkeeper and strengthener of perversion (as the digestive and sustaining belly naturally would be) to empower and enable its wicked cohorts in their evil.

This statuesque body of empires/evil needs the Babylonian head to think and tongue to speak with, the Persian heart and lungs to empower it with life, and the Greek belly with which to sustain, strengthen, and propagate evil. These principalities do work hand-in-glove.

Greece, It's Certainly Not a Health Food

From the time of Adam's first bite of the forbidden fruit, to the last uprising of the heathen at the end of days, the flesh, the natural body and that which affects it, has become the central element in fallen mankind's life. It is this Grecian prince who dominates that third portion of man through his unique position as a purveyor of false hopes and fabricated pleasures unto the fallen flesh.

The fact that this midsection of the body is portrayed as the metal alloy of brass illustrates that the Grecian prince rules an area not as genuinely precious to man as the other two previously mentioned empires of pure metals were. Having said that, brass does slightly resemble gold, which is the precious metal portraying the head, which is ruled by the kingdom of Babylon, the bearer of the curse of confusion and religious self effort.

Yet, the areas of brass are not as critical for the survival of the wicked transgressionary effort as are those of the golden head and the silver heart. The brass belly is very important, but it is not as critical for the essence of this perversion of mankind to exist. For the golden head represents the soul, and the silver arms and breast symbolize the spirit, but the brass belly and loins stand for the flesh, the physical portion of mankind, which, while it is equal in value and purpose to the soul and the spirit, was originally created to serve the other two.

However, since the fall of Adam, this brass area vies with the others for dominant control of subjugated man. Specifically, it seeks to replicate in authority the gold it resembles as it attempts to foist its own "religion", the worship of the flesh and the knowledge of the fallen (un)natural world, upon man through which it hopes to control the entire triune being, and eventually all of creation through it. This is so, despite the fact that the Grecian is based in only one (all too sizeable) area of the statue.

Now, in looking at this brazen prince (Notice the fitting play on words? The word "brazen" can mean both "bold" and "audacious", as well as meaning "brass."), one cannot help but observe that his rule is over the largest area of the statue's trunk. This is in keeping with the very substantial influence that all things physical had, and have, upon the family of man.

This large area of rule is quite appropriate when seen from the perspective of man's fall, for since that time the physical portion of man, the body, has been the one trying to affect and drive the entire will of man. Adam's sin caused the servant (the body) to vie for the right to become the served, and the size of the Grecian's area of rule indicates that the perverted physical nature of man is a strong and tireless contender for the position of the served.

CHARMED... I'M SURE.

In our look at the brass prince of Greece, it cannot be helped but to mention the origins of the name of his metallic empire. The original Aramaic word for brass (and Aramaic is the language this statuesque second chapter of Daniel is said to be written in) that is found in the Book of Daniel is "nechash". It has as a root and relative the Hebrew word "nachash". This word "nachash" means: to practice divination, divine, observe signs, learn by experience, practice fortunetelling, and take as an omen.

Why are these two disparate meanings connected through these closely related words? What is the magnetic attraction between these two seemingly distinct words of "nechash" and "nachash"?

Well, "brass", the Aramaic "nechash", is very reflective when polished, and it was actually a common substance used in the production of mirrors in the middle east of yore. *(Exodus 38:8)*

This shiny, glimmery, and beautifully reflective polished brass (nechash) was a source of fleshly enchantments for all too many people. And, not only in an innocent sense: for divinators, sorcerers, necromancers, and others who fancied various forms of witchery often used the shiny things of brass (the Aramaic nechash) to help them practice and purvey their sorceries (the Hebrew nachash).

This use of such glittery objects by those who fancy witchery is much in keeping with the way the well known and very shiny, glimmery, crystal balls are said to be used in the common wizardry of a more recent vintage.

How does this "charming" explanation tie in with our look at the brass Grecian and his workings explained in these aforementioned linguistic linkages?

Greece, It's Certainly Not a Health Food

As stated, this Grecian is the premier prince of the paunch, the big boss of the belly; in other words, he runs the fief of the flesh. In keeping with that thought, it is the statue's central area of brass (nechash) which he rules and skillfully polishes into a beauty of nearly unreal glitter with which mankind has become thoroughly enchanted (nachash).

The spirit of empire which most powerfully entrances man is clearly the Greek. When Adam's children lock their eyes into a hypnotic gaze while viewing this great and terrible statue, this image of empires, it is their own reflection (deceptively altered in the tummy of terror) shining back at them from the beautifully polished fleshly domain of this Grecian that is most evidently seen. We most easily recognize ourselves, and our own physical lives, in the reflections of the things ruled and affected by the brazen one.

The brazen Greek prince is quite skillful in the art of making the satanic illusions perpetrated by the princely puppeteers of perversion seem real. In other words, the bronzed prince is an expert at using all manner of sorcery and witchcraft to subjugate mankind with the deceitfulness and vanities of the fallen flesh.

Now, this is not to say that the other wicked spiritual principalities are incapable of the same types of misleading behaviors, but the roots of the ways of the fallen flesh today stem from the actions associated with this overbearing prince; and one of the largest of the many twisted stems of the flesh is that of witchery.

Actually, it can be said that all things inherent to the fallen way of life as commonly lived through the flesh is a form of witchcraft. It is perversion, deception, illusion; a false premise for conduct, and a false promise of fulfillment.

This way of witchcraft is the Grecian's grassroots effort (or should we say "brass roots" effort) to hide the truth of God and to attempt a perversion of His will. In this manner, the Grecian hopes to prevent the original, eternal, intent of God from taking place for the creation.

As it has been duly noted, the control of the flesh portion of fallen mankind's existence is the forte of the Greek prince, and all things natural to the "unnatural" existence of fallen man is a perversion of God's reality and a warping of His intentions. It is a wicked satanic enchanting of mankind.

In fact, the Apostle Paul quite clearly states that the so-called overt sorcery, magic, and witchcraft espoused by the more brash elements of the heathen is nothing more than a work of the flesh. Such acts and practices are not "spiritual" in nature as some suppose, nor are they of the soul. They are carnal in nature, and nothing more. It would seem the Grecian prince is the brazen belly firmly entrenched behind all such physical by-products.

Witchery is but a feeble fleshly imitation of a true walk in spiritual matters (it can be seen as brass masquerading as unsullied gold) which only a relationship with God can provide through the rebirth of the spirit of the triune man in the Messiah Jesus.

> "Now the works of the flesh are manifest, which are [these]; Adultery, fornication, uncleanness, lasciviousness, Idolatry, witchcraft, hatred, variance, emulations, wrath, strife, seditions, heresies, Envyings, murders, drunkenness, revellings, and such like...." (Galatians 5:19-21)

ORGAN MUSIC? ...OI, GEVALT!

Once again, as is the case with the previously mentioned principalities, we can learn a great deal about the attributes of this particular principal spirit by looking at what organs are found in his area of the statue. The central area of the body which this prince rules in the false image of man contains many organs. In fact, it contains more organs than any other, but first among them all is the stomach.

The stomach is his greatest simile; the ever hungry, always ready to consume vast quantities of pleasurable items and enlarge itself to no end, stomach. This prince of "gluttony" has the children of Adam running rampant in the pursuit of excess and lusting after nearly everything the physical world allegedly consists of.

The Grecian has mankind focused on perverting and misusing all things in God's creation in all possible ways. In deceit he cries: "The things of the world are so delightful, no expense is too high in attaining them; do what you must do to taste of the pleasures of my world."

As the deafening call of the Grecian echoes in the cavernously empty bellies of a beguiled people the gluttonous stomach of a fallen mankind answers in a rumbling which knows no bounds in its desperate desire to own, and devour, all that which God has ever created. However, like everything in the perverted world of satan, the gluttonous stomach finds its wicked, ever-consuming, actions lead to a twisting and painful knot of raging indigestion which even the strongest of antacids cannot cure.

Everything this angel of excess brings to mankind boils down to a false sense of appetite, a penchant for perversion, and a desperate desire to satiate it. Each unsaved person is trapped within the bloated bowels of the Grecian, and is bound to a countless number of weighty yokes as this errant angel ever seeks to increase the false need in man to attain the unattainable, and to live within the deceptive confines of the ever consumptive flesh at the expense of truth.

The brazen one acts as a manipulator extraordinaire, binding man in the name of pursuing a vanity, a false, unattainable, nonexistent goal and pleasure. The prince of Greece knows that such flesh-corrupting activity destroys the soul and brings death to the spirit, as he seeks to have the fallen flesh rule in the realm of Adam. Human history illustrates that point well.

Such wickedness masquerading as "natural human behavior" is thusly able to ride roughshod over the family of a despoiled mankind and it leaves this dark angel safely enthroned in his principality, ensuring that his twisted power remains uncontested by man's trampled spirit and trodden down soul.

The flesh, which this Grecian seduces with his falsehoods, is then slowly and surely sent to its sin bought grave, leaving the wicked angelic conspirators alone in power as those who would rule defiant of God in this perverted world of death.

Actually, nearly every organ found in the area of control of this brazen angel prince is involved to some degree in either the quest to have or the processing of the obtained. These organs have then been distorted into elements utilized in the corruption, defilement, and perversional tainting of that which has been first used, then wasted, and finally desecrated. The false promise of the Grecian is fulfilled in a person's wasted life of bondage to an infinite array of profane wants and whims. And, that is the exact opposite of God's way of living, which is a seeking to give unto, bless, strengthen, and affirm all life.

The Greek prince of brass has mankind shackled to a huge and very heavy cart laden full of endless sins and needless diversions which Adam's children are manipulated into pulling like beguiled beasts of burden, like deceived donkeys, which are lured into hard service by the promise of a beautiful, but unattainable, carrot dangling on a string right before their noses, but just out of reach. And, satan laughs.

TOO BRAZEN?

AKA

"NOTHING TO ...WHERE!?!"

Yes, the Bible, in stating that both the belly and the thighs were of brass, was ever mindful to inform us in its distinctively subtle and most polite way that it specifically includes the groin with the procreative organs of the image into the area subjected to the wicked prince of Greece. He is the overseer of the fief of the flesh, after all.

And, ever true to his mandate, this brazen Grecian has worked tirelessly to corrupt and deceive mankind through the perverted use and manipulation of those specific organs placed at his disposal, as well as through all others found within his area of rule. The bronze prince is the very epitome of perversion and will use all means in his arsenal to corrupt mankind, especially by warping the issues of life and love into those of lust and defilement.

Every subsequent generation of fallen man ever born is conceived through the means and organs which are found in the Grecian's area of rule. In that way, mankind is sadly subjugated under the weight of the Adamic curse, and under the principalities found in the false standing image of empire, the terrible statue of Nebuchadnezzar's dream.

All of mankind is the fallen Adam's children, and all are born into a sin debt which they can never hope to repay. This brazen spirit of the flesh, this lascivious liege of the loins, is known for his perversional tendencies and lustful lies which he brings to bear upon mankind through the corrupt administration of the organs of the nether regions. The brazen prince does oversee the canton of carnality with the greatest of perversions, after all.

The Grecian is constantly attempting to yoke the children of Adam into all manner of distorted bondages and oppressive burdens, and he uses every organ at his brazen disposal to do so; all in the quest to ruin the holiness of a mankind the satanic conspirators so fear. For man is the being made in God's own image. (*Genesis 1:26-27, 9:6*)

The Grecian also uses the natural and God created gender differences inherent to mankind for the evil benefit of the satanic conspirators by distorting that holy issue which was meant by God to strengthen humanity and to build the family of man.

Each gender was created to bring forth its own particular form of God likeness, a revelation to creation of the uncorrupted character of the Holy God. However, that understanding has also been lost in the reflections of the brass belly as mankind now cowers in the shadows of this, *"terrible"*, image.

One simple way the Greek prince is able to corrupt holiness is by misleading people over how they need to conduct themselves around others. In this manner, he can bring about both defilement and beguilement into the creation. From the instituted lack of basic morals to the implementation of ridiculous religiously based segregation, the world is replete with satanically deployed schemes of culturally induced gender based destruction.

Even within the most well meaning of religious cultures we have the devised segregation of people into specific, and carefully manufactured, "pigeonholes". Religion has developed a contrived "group think" mentality; it is replete with divisions based on physical differences none of which are founded upon spiritual truth. It is: old vs. young, woman vs. man, marrieds vs. singles, ethnic group vs. ethnic group, etc. etc...

In such a way this satanic prince can cause even the most well intentioned people to build "social" barriers between themselves and have them separate from each other. This is devised in order to further divide and conquer the family of Adam so that the different aspects of mankind, each with its own particular blessings, anointings, and authorities could not come together and assist each other in the journey back unto the God of all righteousness. It is the old "divide and conquer" plot at work.

This prince is, indeed, brazen beyond all words.

THE "BELLY" OF THE BEAST
AKA
"GETTING DOWN TO BRASS TACKS"

As is the case with the two previously referred to angel princes, much can be learned about this gastrovascular Grecian by looking at the culture of the nation most influenced by his rule, and that nation is none other than Greece itself (Don't you just love these unexpected surprises?).

Ancient Greece is known as the cradle of democracy (literal meaning: the rule of the people). It was the birthplace of philosophy (literal meaning: the love of wisdom). As a culture, it was enamored with learning and understanding; education was prized, and intelligence highly valued, but the basis of all such Greek wisdom was carnal.

Greece was the nation which first cemented man's adoration of sport; it was the setting of the original Olympic Games where physical exploits were both worshipped and used in the worship of idols. Greece was also the heartland of all manner of gender perversions; its populace was at the forefront of nearly all immoral debauchery of the flesh.

It was also home to the worship of a myriad of false "gods"; many of which had their origins in either a slew of wicked angels, their hybrid human offspring (the nephilim, rephaim, anakim, etc.), or an occasional well thought of human ancestor whose identity and life story was twisted beyond all recognition through the shifting course of time and mind.

The culture of Greece had at its core the pleasing of the flesh and the promotion of the physical; in other words, the culture of Greece could be described as self-centeredness, self-promotion, self-importance, and hedonism. This is in true keeping with the brass bellied position the empire of Greece held within the statue. The people of the nation were apt to perversely love "self" to the near total exclusion of all others.

Loyal to the intent of its reigning principality, the Greek culture was the embodiment of "flesh worship". The natural was everything, the physical all important. Everything was made subservient to the bodily desires native to the unnatural existence of a fallen mankind lost in a satanically contrived world of individualism. Greece was the land that loved the physical.

Do remember now, when discussing the forte of the Grecian prince we aren't necessarily or singularly speaking of the overt acts of wanton sin which many may exclusively associate with the things of the flesh. No, the domain of this prince spirit is over and inclusive of all those things of the flesh which make up the normal everyday life of mankind, debaucherous sins notwithstanding. It is precisely this fact, his ability to design and implement "the norm", which gives the Grecian a place in the terrible statue.

Our longing for wealth or comfort, our adoration of the successful and famous, the importance we place on titles, degrees, and formal education, the cult of celebrity; these are all examples of our everyday lives running towards illusion, and moving contrary to the Word of God. These overt desires, natural to mankind, which seem so normal and good can and do stem from a deception rooted in the ways of the Grecian prince.

It is also important to bear in mind that culture (as epitomized by the highly "refined" Grecian empire) is no indication of civility. Culture, theater, the arts, formally instituted educational facilities and practices; all of these are found in even the most brutal and cruel of nations as they existed throughout the years of history, and all of these perversional places would eagerly lay a stately claim upon the title "civil".

The Bible says the following in Proverbs 14:12:

> "There is a way which seemeth right unto a man, but the end thereof [are] the ways of death."

It is this Greek prince which helps natural man to see what he, "seemeth", to be right.

Unlike its predecessor, Persia, which relied on strength of numbers when it came to warfare, Greece preferred finesse over brute force, battle tactics over sheer numbers.

The small, independent, city states which comprised the Greek nation were often engaged in external warfare with foreign enemies, and even in open hostility and conflict amongst themselves. As such, the Greeks learned to rely upon their love of physical knowledge and technology to give them the edge over their much larger and more "powerful" enemies.

The Greek culture was quite adept at stretching its love of learning into all areas of life, including into the military arena. The Greeks would commonly use creative technology and battlefield ingenuity to make up for the lack of numbers the Greek armies could field.

The armies of Greece, especially during the reign of Alexander, the son of Phillip (reigning 336-323 B.C.), often faced and conquered enemies up to ten times their own number through their use of tactics and technology. This brilliant military machine was another visible form of "the flesh" found flourishing under the Grecian's paunchy rule. Cunning and fortitude won the day many a time for this nation which served the "natural body" as enthusiastically as the repentant should serve his God.

The brazen way in which this empire audaciously stepped in to influence the human arena in thought, culture, and warfare towards its present day state of overt Hellenism is a clear indication of the actions and involvement of the angel prince of Greece as he manipulates life as found in the realm of fallen man.

WE NEED THE "OIL" OF THE HOLY SPIRIT, NOT THE "GREECE" (GREASE) OF THE FLESH

But, praise God! We who are in Messiah Yeshua need not be oppressed by this foreign ruler! We are liberated from the fallen flesh through Jesus' atoning death and we are able to live in the promised peace of Israel's King Messiah! He is the Word of God made Flesh! We need not slave away toiling for a false physical nirvana, the pursuit of which adds misery to misery, and heartache upon heartache, in its broken promises. We have the genuine promise of rest in our Mighty God! Amen!

> "...The LORD [is] my shepherd; I shall not want. He maketh me to lie down in green pastures: he leadeth me beside the still waters. He restoreth my soul..." (Psalm 23:1-3)

CHAPTER NINE

THE ROAMING ROMAN

The fourth prince of empire to come under our inquisitive gaze is none other than the Roman, the strong iron legs of the great night image.

The Roman prince is unique among the rulers of the body part principalities which compose the false image of man in that his empire: the legs, like the iron of which they are composed, are the strongest parts of the body of the statue.

They are the strongest, but they are also the simplest in function. As such, they are not highly valued in comparison to the important contribution they make, just as iron is not highly valued in comparison to the precious and semiprecious metals of which the other afore mentioned body part empires were composed. Iron is the lowest in value and most common of the metals used in the image and well reflects the abundant strength, but small in ability to uniquely alter events itself, principality of Rome.

What is the Roman's job in this metallic personification of princely puppetry known as the great image? Actually, the Roman prince can be simply described as a delivery service for the satanic conspirators. He is a malignant messenger of malice, a crooked courier of corruption, a tireless transporter of tyranny, and an energetic envoy of evil.

The prince of Rome is an enabler of the other empire spirits, and as such, he is well represented by the strong iron legs. In fact, legs contain no organs specific or unique unto them, just as Rome has no real character of its own.

THE KNOCK-OFF ARTIST

The attributes of this empire prince are actually well foreshadowed and explained by the land whose name he carries. This physical Rome was a knock-off artist, an appropriator, it borrowed from other nations and cultures the attributes which best suited itself and wholeheartedly took them for its own.

At times it did so without changing anything about the cultural characteristics it took upon itself, and yet at other times it drastically changed things melding and morphing them freely with other previously usurped characteristics to suit its own purposes or needs. In either case, few of its characteristics were truly of its own design.

Rome's unadmitted mission was to help convey those usurped attributes of previous empires and cultures, both conquered and foreign, but every attribute in question, far and wide, just as a strong pair of steely legs should. The angel prince did precisely the same thing, spreading the wickedness inherent to the other principalities abroad with an enthusiasm few would relish.

Rome, the long iron legs of the statue, had one important job in the great image. As the legs, its job was to carry and spread these three other previously mentioned spirits and their mankind crippling attributes into the entire world of man. This spirit of Rome whose rule was over the natural land of the "empire of the roadway", with its strong iron legs, doesn't stand around long enough to get rusty.

It moves, it marches, it carries the three more precious principalities with it and ensures that their biting yokes are placed and ever present upon Adam's fallen race.

The Roman prince has an iron will to thrust all the evils of the other principalities onto mankind. He will chase down and trample everyone who attempts to avoid or resist the confederation of evil, and he will endeavor to ensure complete human compliance to the devilish designs of the wicked ones as he trounces on the will and subdues the ranks of fallen man.

In that the legs are generally the longest parts of the body it means that the Roman was, and is, set to run as a spiritual power for a long, long, time. Running is what legs do, after all. As the reigning world principality for the last two thousand plus years this iron prince is a marathoner extraordinaire.

The Roman prince is nothing if not the enabler of the others. His authority and power in the world gives the other statued satanic conspirators a venue from which to reach those who dwell in even the farthest and most disparate corners and cultures of the earth as they piggyback upon this ever moving and morphing principality. In essence, the Roman assists the other principalities in their duties while force-spreading their evils into the lives of a satanically subjugated race known as mankind.

It may be commonly thought that the Roman time of rule, symbolized by the two iron legs, was the beginning of the era of division within the statue. However, a closer look at the details given about the terrible statue reveals that the divisional events began in the Greek loins, the thighs, and not in iron legged Rome.

That's one thing loins and thighs do very well actually; they proficiently branch off from the core of the body and transition into individual legs. A glimpse back into history shows us that the brazen prince of Greece began the many divisional traits of existence which were then absorbed and mimicked by the ferrously leggy prince of Rome.

The legs of Rome faithfully continued with the divisions of man's life first seen occurring in the Grecian thighs. The political, economic, cultural, and spiritual aspects of mankind's fallen existence were further refined in this era of Roman rule; eventually reaching their present more refined, but equally sordid states of being.

The deceptions of soulish self effort, spiritual ability, and physical fulfillment are all carried into the lives of man by this power which symbolizes the tireless nature of evil.

The many different facets of wickedness found in this artificial mirage called "normal human life" were separated from each other in order that each may be used in its fullest effectiveness by the conspirators during the chronological, but illogical, sequence of events which played out in the statue of image. And, now the great deception known as "modern civilization" has been fully brought to bear upon those of present day fallen man.

The Empires of Image

From its worship of Babylonian deities and utilization of Babylon's solar based calendar, to its use of the Persian cross and most willing adoption of Persian brutality, through unto its love of Greek "gods", philosophies, knowledge, government, and debaucheries; the physical principality of Rome has faithfully spread the ways of its "ancestor" empires into the world in which we live, in more ways than mankind can possibly conceive of.

Equally so, the convincing spirit known as the prince of Rome has the entire population of the earth thinking that the ways in which the wicked principalities have mankind living life is "normal". It cries: "Anything but the true God." And, it carries with it an eternal jealousy and hatred for the nation of promise, Israel, as it understands the dramatic implications of Israel's redemption and return better than mortal man can imagine.

A "LEG" UP ON ROME

Again, as with the other empires, the best way to further add to our knowledge of the Roman prince's traits of conduct is for us to look at the empire of his rule, Rome itself.

Rome was an amalgam of peoples and ideas. In fact, one would be hard pressed to find a person of true "Roman" extraction within the Roman empire. That same empire freely borrowed and adapted itself to whatever concepts best suited it at any given time in history, which is one reason for its political and physical longevity. This is also why so many Roman concepts are still with us today; albeit, many of them inconspicuously.

Rome practiced Babylonian forms of religion, it epitomized the Persian power lust, and it absorbed and assimilated the Greek culture like no other nation did; in many ways becoming a close cosmopolitan replica of Greece.

Rome, as well represented by the iron legs of the statue, was the most mobile of the ancient empires. It was the first "great power" to build an intricate array of roads and highways throughout its empire in order to expedite the movement of troops, commerce, religions, and ideas with which it could efficiently spread the power and (adopted) concepts of the "Roman" empire throughout the world. Rome, the empire, was also the home of the master politician, raising the way in which all manner of diplomacy and political planning was used to that of an art form. And, so it is unto this day.

The crucifixion, the cunning, the brutality; the perversions leading to outright blaspheme... Rome held the world by the throat, and needed to find a reason not to squeeze. All nations which heard the name "Rome" stood in fear of its strength. This was a power which seemed unstoppable. It was not to be trifled with, not on a physical level or on a spiritual, for Rome held all the cards. Except for one....

DON'T GET TRAMPLED BY THE IRON ROMAN!
AKA
"AVOID THE ROMAN IRON(ING) BOARD"

There was a promise made by a patient and omnipotent God unto His friend Abraham, the Hebrew. That promise simply stated that Abraham's seed was to inherit the earth.

And, Praise God! The Messiah Yeshua (Jesus), the seed of Abraham, of the root of Jesse, from the tribe of Judah came and conquered. We can live in the life of His promise, and not be crushed by this Roman and his legions of iron. Those in the grace of Messiah have been set free from the fearsome ferrous bonds of the iron empire and we can rejoice in God's goodness as we eagerly await the arrival of the soon coming King!

> *"For yet a little while, and he that shall come will come, and will not tarry." (Hebrew 10:37)*

CHAPTER TEN

"A COUPLE OF REAL HEELS?"

AKA

"DANCING THE TWO-STEP"

Our look at the terrible trophy of satanic sabotage wouldn't be complete without a brief inspection of this next well-heeled chap.

This footy fellow is well capable of tripping up even the most careful of people, causing them to stumble if they aren't vigilant. The fifth empire and its prince, is the one which is yet to come, and is the one we naturally have the least information on (it's just difficult to track footprints which haven't actually appeared yet). Its name and definite identity will remain hidden until its physical arrival as the perverse ruler of nations.

However, looking at its place in the statue can give us insight into its role within the spiritual workings of the evil princely angelic image and of its unique ability to oppress a fallen mankind. This fifth empire is portrayed as the iron and clay feet of the terrible statue of image.

Feet, like the legs to which they are so firmly attached, do not contain any vital organs, nor are they critically necessary for the existence of the being in question. Hence, the spiritual similarity between this fifth empire of iron and clay, and the extremely useful, but not absolutely vital for existence, iron legs. Neither is vital for the existence of this evil work.

Alright, for a bit more insight, let's ask the following question:

What exactly do feet accomplish for the body?

Feet help balance the body and keep it upright; they also work with the legs, assisting them to propel the body forward. Feet are also a body's contact point to the earth and the things thereof.

Feet, especially the feet of this statue, are the only parts of a body which are specifically made to contact the ground, and in that way they have a unique ability to enable the other body parts to have access through themselves to the earth. This is another way to stress the weighty importance of the feet (and the angel prince thereof) within the overall image of empires.

The feet carry the iron legs, which connect to the brass lower torso, which supports the silver arms and chest, which bear the golden head. All of the other body part empires are thusly able to pass their massive weight onto the ground, to the earth and the things thereof, through this prince of the feet.

Now, remember, dust is definitively a thing of the earth. And, scripturally it is mankind that is uniquely made from the dust of the earth, a fact which explains how this sure footed fellow brings its weight to bear upon mankind, which is dust pressed upon by the fifth prince of empire. *(Genesis 2:7, 3:19)*

This purported prince of podiatry is, and has always been, far more active in the satanic conspiracy than we could imagine. As the feet, he carries the entire weight of the princely cabal and enables all within to stand, ruling as they have. The prince of feet gives the others the ability to actively affect peoples' lives, both corporately and individually, by bringing the entire weight of evil to bear upon a manipulated and fallen people.

Remember, out of all of the princes in the statue, it is only this surefooted fellow who comes in direct contact with the earth and the things thereof. Importantly, that includes the dust matter of which man is composed. As such, his is the weight which first and fully comes to rest upon the bent and broken backs of the children of fallen Adam.

With his own weight placed firmly atop the lives of man, this fifth prince is then able to press the entire burden of the statue of empire upon those subjugated by satan. This he does in order to convey the weighty wickedness of the others onto an already beaten and bruised race of man.

That is why his time of direct inherited rule has not yet come. Though he has long been active among the others in the "spiritual" arena of subjugation, the fifth prince now operates in a support position subordinate to the presently ruling Rome. Remember now, all spirits of empire have been equally active in mankind's existence since Adam first fell, but they each also have a specific set time of rule.

THE FIFTH PRINCE; TAKING ONE STEP AT A TIME

AKA

"THE INFAMOUS FEAT OF THE FEET"

The coming full rule of empire by this fifth principality will allow for the entire devastating burden of evil found in the statue to be placed upon mankind at one time, and natural man will be helpless against it.

During the rule of this prancing prince the great tribulation will take place. The man of sin, the anti-Christ, will arise; and more of mankind will die through the myriad events of annihilation occurring in the time of his reign than have died during the tenures of any of the previous princes. For the footy fifth prince carries the ability to implement the crushing full weight of the entire metallic image onto the earth.

Notice that this fifth empire is constructed of two very different substances: it is made of both iron and clay. The reasons for this empire to be made of iron have already been looked at previously and are rather self explanatory, mimicking Rome as it shall. But, now let's look at the basis for the existence of miry clay in the feet.

The explanation of the existence of clay in the construct of this particular empire is quite forthright: clay is made of dust and man is made of dust. The clay found within the feet is man. Man has been, and will continue to be, the worst enemy of mankind in history. Nothing has brought more evil to bear upon people than other people. The fact that the clay is seen as an integral part of the feet shows us that the unrepentant of mankind have been fully incorporated into the scheme of the satanic cabal during fallen man's tenure upon the earth, and man will specifically be used by evil during this coming age of the ferrous feet.

So, the clay shows us that man both enables and assists the agents of spiritual wickedness to press their own will onto Adam's children. These unrepentant enablers of evil upon the earth known as "mankind" are well seen placed into the feet of fury as they are among the most effective instruments of sin and subjugation the satanic posse of princes has in use. Since the time of Adam's fall man has been utilized most effectively by the evil angels to harm others of mankind and to bespoil creation. It is a case of molded dust (clay) crushing dust.

"MEASURING; HEAD TO TOE"

In that the feet are the smallest independent area of the great image it means that the time of the fifth prince's rule will also be the shortest of all the ages of empires in the statue. Its time of rule can last anywhere from a minimum (and very probable length) of approximately seven years through to an unidentified maximum.

However, it will almost assuredly physically exist for a shorter chronological duration than the time of reign held by the empire of Babylon. Chronologically speaking, Babylon was the shortest ruling empire within the image to hold sway thus far, and its area of rule, the head, is also notably the second smallest of the body part empires; the iron and clay feet are the smallest body parts in both size and anatomical weight. Ergo, Babylon's time of rule stands as an absolute cap as it towers head and shoulders above the dusty feet in both important categories.

However, we must not let the extremely short tenure of this prince deceive us into a false sense of complacency about its ability to rule, or of its power to do so, which when wielded will be second to that of no other wicked prince. Its tenure may be short, but this prince can go toe-to-toe with any of the others.

As with the divided legs of iron, this kingdom will also be divided into two distinct halves. This is best exemplified by the time of its rule in the seven year tribulation period which is itself composed of two distinctly different three and one-half year periods of time.

These two distinct times can be seen as the individual steps of the two different and individual feet: As the first and weaker foot initially steps onto the earth with authority we can see the beginning of the tribulation period occurring. This is a time when things are, and become, quite bad. However, the events which take place in the first half of the tribulation period are all in preparation for the second and stronger foot to come as it lands with its crushing weight upon the already shaken planet in the second half of the tribulation period.

That second half of the tribulation will be the physical realization of the satanic conspiracy's final attempt to kill, steal, and destroy all things in the physical world created by God. The principality of the iron and clay feet will be the one in whose time all of this coming infamous evil takes place. *(Daniel chapter 12; Matthew 24:21-22; Mark 13:19-20; Revelation chapters 6-20)*

EVEN IF THE SHOE FITS... DON'T WEAR IT!

We do not need to fear the stomping of the satanic shoes as worn by this or any other foe of righteousness, not in this time or in the time to come! Jesus is our Lord and we can rest assured knowing that the evil ones will not tread upon the backs of those made righteous in the grace of Messiah.

The time of wickedness now upon the earth and the time of great tribulation to come are subordinate to the King of Kings who shall guide the lives of those who call upon Him, and we shall be delivered from the hands (and the feet) of the wicked! Amen!

> *"Because thou hast kept the word of my patience, I also will keep thee from the hour of temptation, which shall come upon all the world, to try them that dwell upon the earth." (Revelation 3:10)*

CHAPTER ELEVEN

THE SUMMER IS NIGH

THE ARCHANGEL MICHAEL: A REAL STAND-UP GUY

"And at that time shall Michael stand up, the great prince which standeth for the children of thy people: and there shall be a time of trouble, such as never was since there was a nation [even] to that same time: and at that time thy people shall be delivered, every one that shall be found written in the book."(Daniel 12:1)

As the time of Israel's national banishment from the grace of God comes to a close, and this once and future holy nation is returned unto its place of promise, the earth shall be shaken with the awesome judgments of its sin. In this time of tribulation the wicked princes of empire are removed by the return to prominence of Israel's righteous angel prince, Michael. *(Revelation 12:7-8)*

During this time of the rule of the gentiles, Michael, along with the nation he oversees, has taken a mandated backseat to the conspiratorial princes of the image. That is why it is written, *"...at that time shall Michael stand up"*, for during the ordained time of exile the great prince is ordered quiet and subordinate to many of the actions of the conspirators due to the sins of his nation.

However, as the exile and banishment of Israel has run its course during the great tribulation period Michael shall be empowered once

The Empires of Image

again and shall arise to guide and protect the regathered nation. In doing so, he shall again inherit the rights of preeminent angelic princedom once held by the wicked in their empires of image. This, in turn, leads to the coming of the Messiah unto His people in great power and glory... *(Mark 13:26)*

A STONE'S THROW AWAY

"Thou sawest till that a stone was cut out without hands, which smote the image upon his feet [that were] of iron and clay, and brake them to pieces. Then was the iron, the clay, the brass, the silver, and the gold, broken to pieces together, and became like the chaff of the summer threshingfloors; and the wind carried them away, that no place was found for them: and the stone that smote the image became a great mountain, and filled the whole earth." (Daniel 2:34-35)

"And in the days of these kings shall the God of heaven set up a kingdom, which shall never be destroyed: and the kingdom shall not be left to other people, [but] it shall break in pieces and consume all these kingdoms, and it shall stand for ever." (Daniel 2:44)

After the rise of the fifth and final gentile empire and its subsequent fervent attempts to impose wickedness into the world take place, another entity will appear to utterly destroy the fifth empire of iron and clay.

The new kingdom will be able to destroy the fifth empire due to the footy fifth empire's overstepping attempts at destruction which far exceed its rights to rule. And, in destroying the fifth empire the new kingdom will also destroy all things associated with it, such as the four previous, and still active, allied princely empires of the image. This new and unique kingdom, which shall come to destroy all the gentile powers, will be none other than the repentant and restored nation of Israel as it comes to be ruled by the King Messiah Himself. It will be the kingdom of, *"a stone... cut out without hands"*.

Remember, when discussing the events surrounding the statue we are not speaking of only political issues or of physical occurrences taking place. We are also speaking of the destruction of the spiritual forces which exist behind the physical. We mean the destruction of the great angelic principalities that bind the children of Adam into a sin soaked false manner of existence, one ultimately ruled by satan; an existence which is designed to bring mankind to erroneously serve the satanic conspiracy in a bondage like no other.

The angelic principality which is found to be in authority at the time Messiah comes to re-establish righteousness is the surefooted fifth fellow, this podiatric prince, who is caught in the act of illegally placing the full massive weight of the conspiracy upon the trodden down backs of man, especially upon the then repentant and righteous children of Israel. *(Isaiah chapter 63:7-9)*

As this fifth prince is the one in power at the time of Messiah's arrival it is only fitting that the stone (the Messiah) would come to smite the miry and ferrous feet of the still standing image first, just as the Bible describes. When Messiah does so, all of the other wicked empires whose power rests upon the feet, and whose power the fifth has inherited and brought to bear upon the earth, and who have each worked to subjugate man through their unified illusionary perversion of existence, will collapse and be utterly destroyed. In other words, take out the feet, and the statue of image doesn't have a "leg" to stand on.

Just what is the kingdom that Messiah comes to establish and grow to the point, *"that no place was found for them"* (*"them"* being the wicked empires and their angels)? It is the returned, regathered, and repentant nation of Israel. Through Messiah, God will reinstitute His nation as the head of nations. He will forgive their sins and bring back the children of His dear friend Abraham unto the land which he was promised so very long ago.

We must remember that God is eternal, His Word is eternal, and His will never changes. All of the promises and covenants which God has made to, and with, the patriarchs and children of the House of Israel shall fully come to pass through the coming of the King Messiah, the greater son of King David of Israel; the One who shall institute and implement God's will.

In stating that, *"the kingdom shall not be left to other people"*, and in saying, *"it shall stand for ever"*, the Bible is quite clear about the matter. When God forgives and regathers Israel unto Himself the wicked principalities and the conspiracy which they serve will have been utterly crushed and their yoke of evil will have been eternally removed from upon mankind and from upon the creation of our God.

No other nation (or empire) will ever again rise up to claim the right to reign over the affairs of man. Israel and her King shall eternally rule the earth in righteousness, and mankind will be free to serve the living God; the God in whose image man was first created. *(Luke 1:33; Deuteronomy 32:9)*

THE RETURN BEGINS

The following questions may be posed...

1. Since this is still the "era of the gentiles", and the empires of the standing image retain control in this day, where does that leave the state of Israel which exists today?

2. How are we to see Israel as a regathered sovereign nation during this time of continuing gentile authority?

3. Isn't the very fact that Israel exists today while the world is yet ruled by the gentile powers contradictory?

Very well, those are worthwhile questions to ask...

As proper contrarians let's tackle the third question first:

Israel existing today during this "time of the gentiles" as an independent nation isn't contradictory to the scriptural narrative; it is, in fact, an essential biblical requirement. God is a God of order; as such, the rules and legal requirements which He has established must be adhered to by all. As we have previously seen, He will not even allow Himself to cause an infringement upon His own Word.

Having said that, we need to remember what originally brought the time of gentile rule about. It was the divided Israelite nation's fall into sin and their subsequent captivity under the Babylonian empire; and then under the other four empires of the dread statue.

That fall into captivity was the legal framework which saw the gentile nations receive authority, not only over the things of the earth, but over the nation of Israel as well. Israel was exiled into the shadows of the powers of empire, and they were also driven out by God into all the nations of the earth. Spread out and scattered, the remnants of Israel came under every national gentile authority until the time their banishment was decreed to be passed.

But, how was this amazing God of rules, order, and legal requirements able to regather Israel from among the entire host of the heathen and liberate them to once again live freely in their own independent land?

God had the heathen nations, the gentile powers of the earth; establish a united format which could legally cede that authority back unto Israel. God allowed the gentile nations to form the United Nations, and on November 29, 1947 the nations of the earth gathered together at the U.N. General Assembly and voted to VOLUNTARILY cede Israel its independence! WOW!

The gentiles had to each give up their claims of authority over Israel, and God brought them together into one place where they chose to do so of their own collective accord! The powers of the world came together as one body and chose to set Israel free from their communal rule! And, on May 14, 1948 the independent State of Israel was reborn. ASTOUNDING, isn't it?!

There was no muss, no fuss, and no rough stuff in this remarkable relinquishing of gentile control over Israel. God simply allowed the heathen powers of the earth to gather together of their own free will. He then let them establish the necessary rules of order allowing for the re-creation of the Israelite nation some 2600 years after it was first wiped off the map!

> "The king's heart [is] in the hand of the LORD, [as] the rivers of water: he turneth it whithersoever he will. " (Proverbs 21:1)

That, my friends, is the reason why Israel had to be re-established as an independent nation during this "time of the gentiles". The gentiles had to be present and in power upon the earth in order for them to grant Israel the right to come out from under their shadows. In so doing, order was kept, and Israel's re-establishment was fully legal according to both Godly and manmade law.

Let's put it this way: the gentile nations have held the authority of the world since the fall of Israel, and they need to be present and in power in order to legally relinquish political independence back unto the fallen nation of Israel.

Now for the answer to the second question: Israel, while it is a nation today, and while it is sovereign, has not yet come into the place of its authority. The authority which Israel lacks is that which the arrival of Messiah shall bring. At such a time Israel shall cease to be a democracy and it shall become that which it previously was: a monarchy.

The Messianic monarchy shall completely end the gentile rule of the earth and fully actualize the independence of Israel. The Messiah will complete the regathering of Israel from all nations, and bring to fruition that which was begun by the U.N. (gentile powers) vote in 1947. *(Zechariah 10:8-10)*

So, how should Israel be viewed during this transitional time?

Israel should be seen as a fig tree whose branches are now tender and whose leaves are put forth. In other words, the tree is alive and growing, but it is not yet summer, which is the time for it to bear fruit. *(Matthew 24:32; Mark 13:28)*

> *"For Israel [hath] not [been] forsaken, nor Judah of his God, of the LORD of hosts; though their land was filled with sin against the Holy One of Israel." (Jeremiah 51:5)*

And finally, to answer our first of these three questions: In this time of transition Israel is a sovereign state, but it is not a welcome member of the "world order"; either of that which now exists or of that which shall exist. And, its regathering is taking place under continually difficult circumstances, many of which are dealt unto it by the existing heathen powers. For the existence of Israel (the nation), and the existence of the great heathen powers (the empires of image), are at total odds with each other. However, Israel, in this transitionary time, is still affected by the heathen through the matter of simultaneous co-existence, rather than through complete subjugation.

Furthermore, in order to properly address this question we need to focus, not on the geo-political equation, but upon the spiritual. Israel's re-establishment as an independent nation is needed in order to bring these great empire spirits into a place where they can be judged and removed from office.

The great empires of this statue will all come against the re-gathered Israel, as they have already been doing. But, this will happen specifically during the great seven year tribulation period, when their offensive actions will surpass all legality and enter into illegality. That overstepping illegality will allow God to bring about their judgment and removal from power.

That fact, in turn, sees the authority to administer "everyday life" returned unto Israel and its Messiah, an event whose benefits are best seen in the millennial Kingdom. This will be the onset of the fig tree's "summer". It's a time when the "SON" shines brightest!

CHAPTER TWELVE

BUT WAIT, THERE'S MORE!

GYPPED EGYPT?

There is one great power which was noticeably absent from the statue and its terrible tale, one that was mentioned earlier in this book, and that power is Egypt.

Egypt has a huge role in the biblical narrative, and is spoken of time and time again. Logically speaking, just the geographic proximity of this great power to the nation of Israel should alone warrant its place in the statue of empire.

Add to this the fact that Israel was itself enslaved in Egypt for hundreds of years and one would expect Egypt to hold a position of preeminence in Nebuchadnezzar's nocturnal image of evil. However, this biblical account found in the Book of Daniel is not a manmade story with a seemingly logical Israel centered format; it is a revelation from God about spiritual matters given unto man through Daniel by way of Nebuchadnezzar. As such, the great power of Egypt wasn't shoehorned in where it didn't belong.

Well, what is Egypt's part in things?

The nation of Egypt was an enslaver, a taskmaster which forced others to do that which they did not want to do. Egypt used its great power to bind and oppress those who came into its grip and did its best to shatter their free will. Egypt is a picture of bondage.

The Empires of Image

In many ways the argument can be made that the angelic principality which rules Egypt is the very spirit of bondage itself. It is the one which is seen enslaving every person, and it causes them to do what they do not wish. It imprisons the minds and souls (and often the bodies) of people in its dungeon's of deceit, and none of the enslaved can find a way to free themselves from its oppressive grip.

The question can well be asked: "If Egypt is such a massive power, why isn't it in the statue of empire?"

That's a very good question. The statue is a compilation of those specific heathen powers which had been given the right to universally rule in the lives of fallen man. They were empires by nature, whereas Egypt always remained a nation at heart; that is a pivotal difference. Egypt (bondage) was never given that unique right of global empire; it was never given the right to forcefully rule vast areas of the lives of those who dwell upon the earth. Consequently, it always behaved as a nation would.

Egypt (bondage) came about its power over man due to man's disobedience and subsequent removal from the presence of God, and then through mankind's de facto self-placement under the authorities of the satanic conspirators. Fallen man's natural life may have been manipulated by the five princes, but God never intended for Egypt (bondage) to have an equally dominant control over mankind. From the time of the fall of Adam God had always arranged for a way to bring man out from the bondage of sin's grasp, so that He could further advance His plan of redemption upon the earth and free His beloved creation from all sources of bondage and wickedness.

Actually, Egypt (bondage), though it is great and powerful in the eyes of those it has enslaved and bound, is nothing in stature when compared to the Word of the Lord God of Hosts who has, and always will, free those who call upon Him. God always seeks to have His will implemented upon the earth anywhere man gives Him the opportunity to do so.

In times past, God freed the children of Israel from the physical power of Egypt. He will similarly free all those who call upon Him and repent from the sins which brought them into their own Egypt (bondage), that which wrongfully enslaves Adam's children upon this earth. This Egypt (bondage) which is so overbearing and powerful in the eyes of those it oppresses has actually been dealt with by God and defeated at the cross of

Calvary through the sacrifice of Messiah. All the individual needs to do is to repent (turn) from their sins, accept the Lordship of Messiah, and call upon the Lord for salvation.

Now, the strength of Egypt (bondage) lies in the sin of man which the other satanic conspirators (both those found in the statue, as well as all others) are able to bring about through the implementation of wickedness. The Egyptian prince is then able to enslave those who have broken fellowship with God and walked away from His will.

It is the job of the other angelic princely purveyors of pain to foist upon mankind the myriad connivances they have available to them which lead man into sin, and once man has sinned, the principality of Egypt (bondage) can then place the shackles of bondage upon the sinner. The Egyptian (binder) moves in as a result of man's acquiescence to the lies of the others.

The five princes of empire instigate and control the corrupted version of "normal" life that man deals with everyday and the Egyptian (binder) gains the right to implement his bondage upon man through the way mankind lives its perverted natural life as designed by the, "*terrible*", five. In other words, the five great princes steer man into prison and Egypt is the jailer.

PASSOVER!

It cannot be overemphasized that Egypt's power to bind man is only applicable through the power of sin over man, and the power of sin is nonexistent for those who accept the gracious salvation offered by God in the Passover Lamb: the sinless Messiah Yeshua in whom true freedom is found from all the works of the evil ones!

> "[There is] therefore now no condemnation to them which are in Christ Jesus, who walk not after the flesh, but after the Spirit." (Romans 8:1)

> "I [am] the LORD thy God, which have brought thee out of the land of Egypt, out of the house of bondage." (Exodus 20:2)

CHAPTER THIRTEEN

HEADS UP!

"And there appeared another wonder in heaven; and behold a great red dragon, having seven heads and ten horns, and seven crowns upon his heads." (Revelation 12:3)

These seven heads spoken of in Revelation 12:3, are clearly those of the dragon; are they not?

This dragon is unmistakably satan. *(Revelation 12:9, 20:2)*

The seven heads are the seven principal spirits which guide and lead the "body" of satan in its actions. That is all quite common sense; guiding and leading are the roles of a head after all (or seven heads in this case). But, how does this all tie in to our look at Nebuchadnezzar's terrible standing night image?

Well, as we have seen, each of these seven heads has its own role, its own specific job to do, as it were. Each, with its own brain, mouth, eyes, ears, nose, etc. is capable of upholding the dragon (satan) on its own and leading it in ample works of evil. In that there are seven heads visible we are not being shown a dragonesque redundancy, but rather the unique functioning of each head working for the good of the whole.

In one level of interpretation (the one we have been looking at), these heads are the five empire spirits of Nebuchadnezzar's dream and their two co-operative cohorts, the national princes of Assyria (the tool of God's judgment) and Egypt (bondage), both of which arose to punish, oppress, or hold Israel in captivity and bondage for a time.

The spirits of Babylon, Persia, Greece, Rome, the fifth empire, Assyria, and Egypt make up the heads of the great red dragon, those which are at war in every way possible with the will of God and the nation destined to truly rule the earth according to that will; the nation of Israel.

Imagine that! So prominent was the influence and the power of these five world dominating empires and their two national cohorts that their principal spirits are considered to be the very heads of satan.

Now, the existence of this monstrous beast and its time of rule will come to a furious end when the King of Israel returns to re-establish the fallen tabernacle of David. *(Amos 9:11)*

This great King Messiah will then smite the dragon that is in the sea (of men) *(Isaiah 27:1)*, and bring to a close the story of the evil one which sought to rule the earth according to his own design. This brings to an end the longstanding and infamous, *time(s) of the gentiles*. Heathen rule will have reached its, *"fulness"*, of time.

Yes, the phrase, *"fulness of the gentiles"*, as found in the writings of the apostle Paul in Romans 11:25 has often been thought to refer to a good thing, which would be the full number of gentile souls coming to know Messiah as Lord in this pre-tribulation age, but that is not the case. A mixing of concepts has occurred in common theology which has considered the regularly used religious term "age of grace" to be synonymous with the scriptural words, *"fulness of the gentiles"*.

The extra-scriptural term "age of grace" is commonly used to define the period of time from the crucifixion of Yeshua (Jesus) unto the beginning of the great seven year tribulation. It is a time when salvation is freely granted unto all who would believe in the Lordship of Yeshua, accept Him as the King Messiah, and repent of their sins.

Whereas, the biblical term, *"fulness of the gentiles"*, is actually nearly synonymous with the other biblical term, *"time(s) of the gentiles*. The term, *"fulness of the gentiles"* refers to the fulfillment (end, completion) of the time in which the heathen nations have ruled over the earth. It is the completion of an era when God's nation of Israel was effectively made subservient to natural man's own sinful will.

This gentile time period began upon the destruction of Solomon's Temple, and it lasts through to the end of the great seven year tribulation. At that time, Israel shall have the rule of all things returned unto itself through the coming of the King Messiah who shall return power unto Jerusalem.

So, these two related terms: *"the fulness of the gentiles"* and, *"the time(s) of the gentiles"*, and the commonly used saying "the age of grace" while having a long overlapping period of time, are definitely not speaking of the same things.

"And they shall fall by the edge of the sword, and shall be led away captive into all nations: and Jerusalem shall be trodden down of the Gentiles, until the times of the Gentiles be fulfilled."(Luke 21:24)

TWO ARE FORGVEN, AND IT'S A TRIPLE BLESSING

Now, an interesting thing about this seven headed dragon, the Bible has amply shown us the destruction of the five empires, and the utter ends of their principal spirits; but, what of the fate of the two nations in this ungodly construct of evil? What happens to Assyria and Egypt, God's judgments having run their course?

Worthy questions, I must say... The five empires will indeed be destroyed, as will all seven ungodly angelic princes, but these two wayward nations will be shown an immense kindness and grace.

As unbelievable as it may seem, these two self-serving and wicked nations will find grace in God's sight. They never became "world empires" and, more importantly, they allowed Israel to live and even increase while she was under their authorities. So, they will have places of honor in the Millennial age, sans their principal spirits, of course. *(Isaiah 19:21-25)*

> *"In that day shall Israel be the third with Egypt and with Assyria, [even] a blessing in the midst of the land: Whom the LORD of hosts shall bless, saying, Blessed [be] Egypt my people, and Assyria the work of my hands, and Israel mine inheritance." (Isaiah 19:24-25)*

When the destruction of this image of empires is complete, at the dawn of the Messianic age, the populace of the earth shall have been freed

The Empires of Image

from the unique yokes of tyranny that each empire and their confederate spirits brought upon man.

SUMMING UP THE PARTS

A short definition of the attributes held by each spirit follows, along with a synopsis of life without their evil effects:

- Babylon: Confusion, the desire for self-attained righteousness. With the Babylonian destroyed, the head of man becomes clear and the soul is free to be itself. Man receives a proper understanding of God, redemption, and the creation; and of man's place within it.

- Persia: Illusion of ability, resistance to God, a trust in all self-effort. The destruction of the Persian brings about a mankind which is free to love the Lord and to fully accept His love. There shall be no more desire in mankind to illogically resist the will of the Almighty.

- Greece: Lust, the desires for the physical world. As the destruction of the Grecian takes place man is no longer driven by vain desires which can never satisfy. Humanity is free to live in God's rest and fulfillment.

- Rome: The power of wickedness; the strength of evil. As this empire spirit is disposed of the wickedness of the others has no way to spread itself upon humanity.

- The fifth empire: Implementation of evil. The annihilation of this principal spirit will see the yoke of satanic lies and bondage removed from Adam's race; the pressing need to sin and follow the falsehoods of satan will be removed from mankind.

THE MESSIAH AND ISRAEL; HAND IN GLOVE

The great Messianic age of the millennial kingdom will see the return and implementation of God's enacted will upon the earth through the restoration of the Kingdom of Israel in Messiah Jesus. This regathering of the nation and its recommitment unto God will return the Adamic blessing and way of life unto the entire planet.

In doing so, the Kingdom and King of Israel, Yeshua (Jesus), will rule in the full office of man as the "second Adam", the sole authority upon the earth. Yeshua shall sanctify the very place which the original Adam had sullied, and He shall restore the Edenic state to the earth; the very same which was lost so long ago. *(Isaiah 11; Micah 4; Zechariah 14:16-21; Revelation 20:2-8)*

The centrality of Israel within the biblical narrative cannot be overstated, nor can the centrality of the Messiah within Israel be overstated. Israel and the Messiah are the very focal points of all earth based Scripture; they are the hope which we have all been given, and they are the earnest gift of promise from God unto creation. It is a promise that shall be fulfilled without any hesitation.

> *"For ye have need of patience, that, after ye have done the will of God, ye might receive the promise. For yet a little while, and he that shall come will come, and will not tarry."* *(Hebrews 10:36-37)*

THE NATIONAL TREASURES

And what of the national form of government which God Himself created and set in motion within the family of man? What becomes of the nations of the earth in the world to come?

As with everything created by the Lord God, the nations are an eternal construct. In the coming Kingdom of our God when the new Jerusalem shall come down from the heavens to rest upon the earth in the eternal age of the "world to come" there will still be unique nations in the family of man. *(Revelation 13:4, 21:2)*

In fact, the book of Revelation makes clear reference to the nations as it describes the eternal coming age:

> *"And the nations of them which are saved shall walk in the light of it: and the kings of the earth do bring their glory and honour into it."* *(Revelation 21:24)*

> *"And they shall bring the glory and honour of the nations into it."* *(Revelation 21:26)*

> "And he shewed me a pure river of water of life, clear as crystal, proceeding out of the throne of God and of the Lamb. In the midst of the street of it, and on either side of the river, [was there] the tree of life, which bare twelve [manner of] fruits, [and] yielded her fruit every month: and the leaves of the tree [were] for the healing of the nations." *(Revelation 22:1-2)*

CHOOSE LIFE

Well, we have looked at the evil which seeks to rule man; we have seen the oppression and the oppressors, and we have contemplated the results of our collective sin. We have also delved into the structures of wickedness which have sought to subjugate and destroy a once graceful mankind. And, we have seen how a kind and merciful God is continually working to restore holiness to the earth by removing all evil.

However, the questions are now put to you, dear reader:

Will you allow a perverted lie called "normal everyday life" continue to bind you and lead you into a satanically inspired quagmire of unspeakable proportions?

Will you continue to allow yourself to be lead towards a life of darkness in the empires of evil, or will you turn unto God and repent?

Will you cry out for His mercy?

Will you humble yourself unto Yeshua (Jesus), the King Messiah; the one who has paid a great price to set you free from all tyranny and oppression?

Will you make Yeshua your Messiah ; will you make Jesus your Lord?

The choice is yours to make...

Choose life, that you and your house may live! *(Deuteronomy 30:19)*

SHALOM

Look for more books, products, and information from:

T. M. Kymalainen

and

Time to Return Ministries LLC.

Visit our website at: www.timetoreturnministries.com

Or e-mail us at: timetoreturn@gmail.com